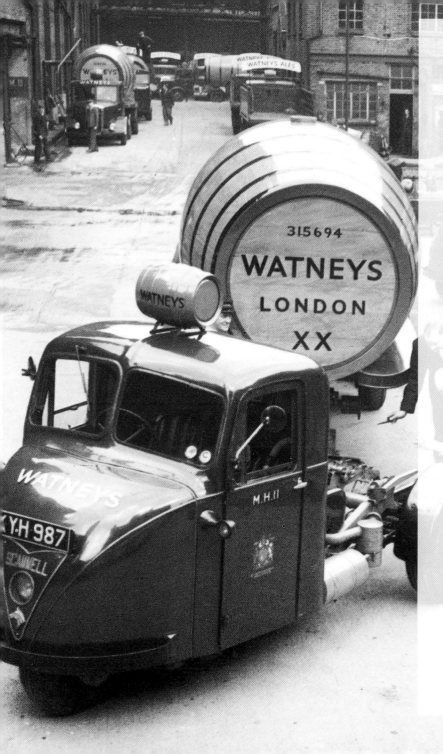

Mechanical Horses

Bill Aldridge

Trans-Pennine Publishing

in conjunction with
The Mechanical Horse Society

CONTENTS

Front Cover: *Three generations of Scammell tractors seen at the former York Goods Depot, now part of the National Railway Museum. All three types of vehicle would have worked here during the depot's life. Alan Earnshaw*

Rear Cover Top: *A Bedford TK 10/12-ton demonstrator articulated tractor seen in its rightful place coupled to a dropside trailer. Vauxhall Motors.*

Rear Cover Bottom: *British Road Services operated a number of 3 and 6 ton Scammell Scarabs within the Parcels Service. This is a 6-ton version. B. Madeley*

Title Page: *A new Scammell Scarab with its barrel trailer is inspected at Watney's Mortlake brewery, April 1954 Mechanical Horse Club*

This Page: *An ex-RAF Scammell Mechanical Horse, in the service of the Grimsby Ice Company, before conversion to battery-electric operation.*

The **Nostalgia Road** Series ™
is conceived, designed and published
by
Trans-Pennine Publishing Ltd.
PO Box 10
Appleby-in-Westmorland
Cumbria, CA16 6FA
Tel. 017683 51053
Fax. 017683 53558
ISDN. 017683 53684
e-mail trans.pennine@virgin.net
(A Quality Guild registered company)

Produced in conjunction with
The Mechanical Horse Club
2, The Poplars, Horsham, West Sussex, RH13 5RH
Tel/FAX. 01403 248188

Reprographics
Barnabus Design & Repro
Threemilestone, Truro
Cornwall, TR4 9AN
01872 241185

And Printed in Cumbria by
Kent Valley Colour Printers Ltd.
Shap Road Industrial Estate
Kendal, Cumbria LA9 6NZ
01539 741344

INTRODUCTION

Ask any modern transport manager about the significance of Mechanical Horses, the London Midland & Scottish Railway, Karrier Motors and the town of Huddersfield, and you will probably get a blank stare. Yet it was the combination of these factors that led to one of the most important and fundamental principles of road haulage today, the articulated lorry.

The Mechanical Horse of the 1930s may seem a long way from today's modern tractor and trailer units, but it was a unique answer to a serious problem encountered by one of the major providers of goods delivery services in the years between the two world wars. The provider of this delivery service was none other than the LMS Railway, and they had wanted to mechanise their town cartage operation by replacing the outdated horse and dray. The problem was that there were no suitable, highly manoeuvrable petrol-driven vehicles that could undertake this type of delivery work. Undaunted this company set out to design their own vehicle, and it chose a small petrol-engined tractor unit to work with its existing fleet of horse-drawn trailers - in other words an articulated lorry.

Above: This line up brand of new LMS Karrier Cob tractors await delivery. The fleet numbers range between 1165G and 1179G from the vehicles visible in the picture. Courtesy P. Newman

Although articulated vehicles were an established concept by the late-1920s they were essentially heavy-duty vehicles designed either to carry large loads over long distances or to transport abnormal loads and there were no contemporary small articulated vehicles. In fact the transport world in general and the medium-size vehicle-user in particular were well catered for by the smaller rigid commercials or indeed by the ubiquitous horse and cart. However, there was one group of companies within the United Kingdom that were quite forward thinking as far as new concepts in land transport were concerned. These were the 'Big Four' railway companies that had been formed in 1923 as a halfway measure to the railway/transport nationalisation that had been promoted at the end of World War I in 1918. These four companies were the amalgam of 118 smaller railway companies that had existed before the war, and between them they offered a full nation-wide goods delivery service for everything from a packet of needles to an industrial transformer.

The railway companies were always looking at better ways of handling freight traffic; their thinking being stimulated by the inrush of new road haulage companies after World War I who threatened their livelihood. Accordingly, the railway companies pioneered the small-articulated vehicle concept as a partial response to the attack on their road haulage interests. Interestingly it was also due to the railways that the medium sized articulated vehicle came to be so important in the post World War II era, and their developments led to the wholesale introduction of articulated vehicles. In fact these vehicles so dominate current road transport, that they have in turn mostly displaced the railway from its original concept as a carrier of goods. This book sets out the story of the introduction of the Mechanical Horse, how it grew to become an essential component in the production line of many factories and how the concept moved into the road haulage industry.

Below: The common perspective of a mechanical horse is the archetypical 3-wheeler like the Karrier Cob, the Scammell MH or Scarab, but 4-wheel vehicles were also very common. One of the most popular types was the Bedford Scammell. Here we see a fleet of Bedford tractors used by the wholesale grocers, Henry Kingham of Watford in 1950. Vauxhall Motors

This book has been written as a sequel to a small booklet produced by the Mechanical Horse Club some years ago. The achievement of the booklet in outlining the history and success of the Mechanical Horses led to the requirement for an updated and slightly larger volume. It is hoped that this latest offering, produced in the highly popular **Nostalgia Road** range will be of interest to both the layman and the enthusiast alike. It is intended that it will also supplement the earlier book and give far more details on the use of the Scammell Automatic Coupling in haulage and industry, as well as giving further details on the vehicles involved.

The expression 'Mechanical Horse' is used to describe exactly what they were; a mechanised replacement for the four-legged horse, operating in conjunction with specially designed semi-trailers. Closely allied with the mechanical horse was the automatic coupling, which again describes precisely the process of attaching the tractor unit to the articulated semi trailer. In this book I have tried to explain how the terms originated, what the vehicles were, how they worked and the uses they were put to, and finally why the system fell from favour.

Bill Aldridge.
Stockport. February 2000.

CHAPTER 1. EARLY THOUGHTS

This is a story that has a beginning, middle and an end, but to start at the beginning, some explanations are required. An articulated vehicle (tractor and trailer) consists of a powered drawing unit with the front of the load-carrying trailer superimposed on the drawing/tractor unit. It is not a new concept, as the first recorded British load-carrying articulated unit was a 3-wheeled steam tractor built in London by a company called Perkins & Sons in the early 1870s. In Paris, De Dion Bouton produced a form of load carrying articulated tractor in 1894.

Perhaps the most well known early British articulated combination was a Thornycroft design of 1898 comprising of a steam tractor and 5-ton trailer, relying on a very basic semi-permanent link between tractor and trailer. While this vehicle was able to demonstrate the improved manoeuvrability of an articulated combination, it was not a success! In the early 1900s two designs of British steam-driven tractor were built to fit directly onto a horse-drawn waggon's front axle, but these were not successful either.

Above: *A view of LMS cartage in the early 1920s, showing horse drays working beside Leyland motor drays.* LMS Official

The problem of how to allow relative movement between tractor and semi-trailer was largely solved with the American designed 'Martin Rocking 5th wheel' in 1909. This device was fitted to a Knox Martin 3-wheel tractor driven by a 40hp petrol engine.

Just before World War I a small number of heavy duty American-built Knox articulated combinations were imported into Britain by the firm of E. W. Rudd Ltd. In this instance the tractor unit was a 4-wheel version of the earlier vehicle and came complete with two or three trailers, each of which were fitted with rubbing plates and landing legs. This enabled the tractor and articulated trailer to be separated, and thus allow for the trailers to be exchanged. The tractor unit was also fitted with a rubbing plate (in modern parlance a fifth wheel) and a kingpin, and the whole assembly was mounted directly on the rear axle of the tractor unit. This enabled the tractor's chassis frame to be much lighter since it carried none of the payload and was separately mounted on the rear axle.

Despite what was quite advanced engineering for the time, physically attaching or detaching the two components was very difficult under anything but perfect conditions. These Knox tractors were later used during World War I as articulated tank transporters and at some point they also came to be operated by the Great Western Railway (GWR). The next recorded complete articulated outfit was produced by Lacre's of Letchworth in 1918 and consisted of a standard haulage vehicle combined with a small trailer.

It was very similar in concept to the Knox articulated vehicle that G. Scammell & Nephew of Spitalfields in East London adopted for their famous 'articulated six wheeler' of 1919. Here the advantage of articulation was not the easily detachable trailer, but 'the additional payload available at nominal extra cost.' Hence in the advertising of the time '7 tons carrying capacity at 3-tons cost and speed.'. Almost as important was the fact that the taxation on this type of vehicle was lower than the tax for the equivalent rigid 6-wheel lorry.

This issue of taxation was based on the fact that the newly formed Ministry of Transport decided that any articulated outfits could be classed as single units rather than a tractor and trailer combination. There was a restriction placed on this new idea in that axle-loading for the third axle should not exceed 6-tons. Yet, as long as the unladen weight of this articulated unit did not exceed 5-tons it could travel at a maximum speed of 12mph and under the traffic regulations of the day, it was also able to tow a trailer giving a payload potential of 13½-tons.

Similar articulated couplings were also adopted by other UK manufacturers for the same benefits, one of these firms was Carrimore, which later became part of the G. Scammell & Nephew group. Despite the obvious advantages of this concept, growth in the articulated market was very slow up till the 1930s with the exception of the rather specialised areas of bulk liquid haulage, machinery transportation and heavy haulage using low-loaders.

Top Left: *Another view of an LMS goods yard, circa 1928, showing the conditions in which road vehicles were having to operate in the period after World War I. Loaded and empty drays can be seen awaiting horses. Yet this yard is relatively 'high tech', as it is provided with a Goliath travelling overhead crane to effect transfer between rail and road wagons.* LMS Official

Centre Left: *Where heavier loads needed to be moved over longer distances many of the railway companies utilised road converted agricultural tractors, in this case an early L&YR International is shown hauling bales of wool into a goods yard.* LMS (L&YR) Official

Bottom Left: *The railway companies had to carry whatever loads they were offered. This LMS chain drive Scammell with a machinery-carrying trailer is typical of the heavier end of the delivery operation. This particular vehicle UR 6305 (fleet no. 1931-B) was allocated to the Manchester area, and it is seen here hauling a formidable looking load from the General Engineering Company at Station Road, Radcliffe.* LMS Official

CHAPTER 2. THE KARRIER CONTRIBUTION

As we have already indicated, the next milestone in the articulation saga came not from the truck manufacturers, but from the London Midland & Scottish Railway (LMS). In common with its three major contemporaries, the London & North Eastern Railway (LNER), Great Western Railway (GWR) and Southern Railway (SR), the LMS were busy replacing the horse and cart with petrol-engined lorries and vans on many duties. The railway road vehicle operation, carrying out the function of collecting and delivering goods to and from the stations had become very important with the railway companies.

All of these public companies offered (between them) a truly nation-wide collection and delivery service for all types of goods. The companies operated a large fleet of small vans for the express parcel deliveries and alongside this was an extensive fleet of lorries and vans in the 2-to 4-ton range, and these were utilised both for the movement of heavier items and on the longer rural delivery routes. The service worked from about 4,700 stations and depots and made use of around 18,000 horses and about 30,000 attendant drays, in addition to the large number of motor vehicles already in use.

Above: *Pictured near the Wolverton Works of the LMS Railway, we see an early Karrier Cob being used in evaluation trials. The vehicle was being tried with a 'Wolverton' style coupling on an ex-horse dray (No.3394) in May 1933.* LMS Official

The railway companies' problem lay in finding a suitable replacement to take the place of the horse on town deliveries and collections. This was an extensive operation generally described as 'town cartage' and one that delivered at least 70% of all commercial traffic in Britain's towns and cities. For this work the horse and dray was almost irreplaceable. Their basic manoeuvrability in the restricted confines of railway depots and town centres (with their poor access for deliveries into shop and factory premises) was a difficult act to follow.

Yet this was the only option for the delivery of most consumer goods, because of the comprehensive network of railway routes (with depots spread right across the country) there were few competing long distance road delivery routes. As a result local road haulage services were few and far between, and the railway held the monopoly. Their collection and delivery network was simply a multitude of many short journeys to and from the rail depots.

This was the type of work ideally suited to the horse and dray, with the empty and full drays being exchanged at the depots perhaps three and four times within a shift, with the horse simply transferring between drays. The railway companies realised that this operation was crying out to be mechanised yet the only road vehicles available from the existing manufacturers were either fairly lightweight or, at the other end of the scale, were the sturdily-built medium to heavy duty load carriers. None of these vehicles offered the required manoeuvrability nor any suitable means of quickly and simply exchanging empty or loaded trailers and this consequently made the search for replacements for the horse fraught with difficulties.

With the undoubted benefit of hindsight it is fascinating to realise that the whole sundries operation (i.e. small parcel deliveries/less than wagonload traffic) was (on its own) a loss-maker for the railway industry. Yet the road collection and delivery was never called upon to make a profit, it was simply there to feed goods onto the railway, but even then with the multitude of depots involved there was little possibility of sending goods directly between depots. There were regular traffic flows that did benefit from direct links, generally the radial routes from London and other city to city links, but overall the service was slow. In addition the basic rates charged were based on the value of the goods carried. Because the rates had to be published it meant that the entrepreneurial road haulier could cream off the better paying traffics and leave the low value goods with the railway. In order to survive the railways had to both improve efficiency, and reduce operating costs!

Almost from the entry into service of the first mechanically driven vehicle the railway companies had experimented with better ways to use them or quicker ways to load them. The railway companies were experimenting with battery electric vehicles as early as 1904 and with demountable bodies a decade or so later. The Lancashire & Yorkshire Railway, for example, had already introduced American towing tractors to assist horses in a number of busy goods yards as shown on page 6.

Top Left: *A Knox tractor adapted by the Great Western Railway at Swindon and provided with a very basic turntable above the rear axle upon which the Swindon-made trailer would be superimposed.*

Centre Left: *With the railways' expertise in manufacturing steam locomotives, it may be considered strange that steam-powered road vehicles were not widely adopted for the railways' road operations. Some railways, like the North Eastern did have a significant fleet of steamers, and one such is this Londonderry Steam Wagon (builders' No. 41) pictured in the York area on 5th April 1911.* British Railways

Bottom Left: *As an alternative to the use of horse drays, with their advantages in the rapidity of exchange, some railways experimented with the use of rigid lorries with demountable bodies. One example is seen here at the GWR's South Lambeth Depot, where rollers transfer the demountable body on to the waiting Burford lorry.*
Buckinghamshire Railway Centre

Above: *The LMS demountable dray system, offering transfer of the platform body from the AEC 5-ton lorry to the horse dray.* LMS

During World War I a substantial number of railway horses and drays were requisitioned by the military, with usually the better examples being taken. By December 1914 around 12% of the railway horses, drays, carts and lurries [sic] had been despatched to the British Expeditionary Force. In the years that followed there was a constant demand for even more, and up to around 50% of all such railway equipment was taken over by the armed forces. Very little of this equipment was returned to the railways after the Armistice.

From 1919 onwards the railway companies did manage to secure large numbers of war surplus lorries from both the British and American forces. These were mainly employed on rural duties, and the remaining horses concentrated on town cartage. Mind you, it should be said that at the time of the Grouping there were over 50,000 horses employed on railway work and their replacement was not going to be an overnight exercise..

During the difficult years of the 1920s, with the slump in trade, the General Strike, and other factors affecting the amount of traffic being moved by the railway, the horse operation was seen to be an increasing liability. It was therefore no real surprise when Mr. J. Shearman, the LMS Railway's Road Motor Engineer, instigated exercises to design a practical petrol-driven vehicle to replace the horse and meet the needs of the 1930s.

His 1929 dictum was that the replacement vehicle would have to manoeuvre as freely as a horse in confined areas. Other requirements included a simple design, a reasonable maximum speed and low maintenance and running costs. A few very experimental models had previously been offered to the railways and tested without much success, including the Autohorse which was a one wheeled self-contained power unit which could attach itself to the shafts of existing horse drawn vehicles. It is possible that the LMS management had also read about the American 'Bulley' towing tractor which was a 3-wheeled tractor that could haul loaded 7-ton trailers in railroad yards when substituted for horses.

In 1929 the LMS Carriage and Wagon Works at Wolverton in Buckinghamshire were given the task of putting the management's ideas into practice. Their first effort was to modify an old Morris Cowley car chassis to form the basic power unit of the articulated combination with a converted horse dray for the trailer. Whilst the idea gave very basic information on the power necessary for the project to work, neither the manoeuvrability nor the coupling operation worked within the required parameters.

Above: *The Wolverton trailer experiments are well illustrated in these two images taken in the Spring of 1933. The upper view shows a 3¼-ton LMS horse dray, No.22044 (to Diagram 87) outside the offices on the Wolverton shop floor. It shows the initial conversion of the front end, where the horse shafts and front axle have been removed from the turntable and replaced with the Wolverton-type coupling and landing legs. The vehicle however retains its standard rear axle and traditional wooden dray wheels.* LMS Official

Below: *The difficulty with the conversion, as seen above, was found by the failure of the drays in service. The wooden wheels, now being drawn at higher speeds, were found to be failing (and in some cases even collapsing) in service. Therefore modifications were introduced to improve the rear end, and the most obvious change was the introduction of an axle fitted with pneumatic tyres. An improvement was also made to the springing on the trailer, and the photograph reveals associated strengthening of the underframe.* LMS Official

The engineers then borrowed a Roberts battery-electric station platform truck. With its short wheelbase and the single front wheel's ability to turn through 180 degrees, the little 3-wheel truck gave the required level of manoeuvrability, but again neither the coupling gear nor the motive power was suitable for the job in hand. The railway company had no wish to be involved in truck manufacture and contacted some of their regular suppliers to see if they could help in supplying small 3-wheeled lorries.

During World War I, Mr. Shearman had been closely involved with Karrier Motors of Huddersfield and he had then purchased many vehicles of this make during the 1920s for the railway. An approach was therefore made to Karrier's head office, where it was found that they had recently introduced a small, short wheelbase, petrol-engined 3-wheeler rigid vehicle for use in restricted areas. The initiative for this vehicle had come from Huddersfield Corporation who required a small dustcart for use in the restricted narrow streets and ginnels of the town.

The prototype dustcart named the 'Colt' entered service in mid-1929 and featured tiny wheels with solid tyres to give a low loading height. The LMS liked what they saw, so the engineers asked Karrier Motors to supply one chassis for experimental purposes. The Karrier Company agreed to supply a 'Colt' chassis for this purpose and offered favourable purchase terms in return for permission to develop a specific Karrier version of the tractor unit.

The commercial potential of this new concept was still an unknown factor, though it was a safe bet that whatever the LMS proposed the other railway companies would follow. Even so, we have to remember that the mechanical horse was a cost-saving exercise, this situation was made even more acute by the Wall Street Crash in October 1929. Because of the quite considerable expense of the new tractor units for town cartage use, the LMS wished to keep the overall cost of mechanisation as low as possible. Naturally they wanted to utilise their large existing stock of horse drays in conjunction with the new tractor units, basically exchanging horses for mechanical horses.

The company management were unwilling to purchase new purpose-built trailers so the coupling equipment had to be designed to work with the existing wooden drays. However, this posed quite a problem for the Karrier design team who were more than aware that the proposition to continue using the old horse drays with these new articulated tractors was less than sound. The vehicle's designers had intended to have their own purpose built trailer, but in view of the determination of the LMS to continue using horse drays Karrier's were forced to develop their own design of a manual mechanism for attaching unmodified horse drays.

At this time the LMS had envisaged modifying the basic Karrier chassis at its Wolverton works purely for its own requirements, and developed a hand-pumped hydraulic mechanism for coupling the existing horse drays to the new 3-wheeled tractor unit. The old horse drays were modified by the simple expedient of removing the horse shafts!

To couple up, the prototype tractor unit was reversed under the trailer where a set of jaws gripped the dray's front axle. The driver then had to hand pump the hydraulic rams that worked a parallelogram style linkage to lift the dray's front axle directly up and over the tractor's rear axle where a large clip held the two parts together. The LMS engineers working on the 'belt and braces' principle had also built a tractor/trailer coupling that was more or less automatic in operation. This became known as the 'Wolverton coupling' after the works that designed it. For this coupling an entirely new turntable fore-carriage was constructed for the trailer.

This carried supporting wheels on brackets that extended outside the tractors' rear wheels. Under the fore-carriage turntable was a set of small rollers that lined up with inverted 'U' channels on the tractor unit. The tractor would reverse under the trailer, and the small runner wheels would engage with the channels. As the tractor continued to reverse the front of the trailer would lift off the ground and a large hook completed the coupling operation. The slope of the ramps on the tractor provided sufficient lift to give the supporting wheels clearance when coupled to the tractor. The coupling operation had become almost fully automatic; the only manual operation was for the driver to insert locking pins into the forecarriage. This coupling was (to some extent) designed to fit newly-built trailers and was really totally unsuitable for the thousands of old horse drays that the LMS planned using in conjunction with the Karrier model.

All of these original 3-wheel tractor units made use of very small solid tyres like the rigid prototype. In the case of the rigid dustcart, such wheels being dictated by the minimum loading height, in the tractor's case the LMS requirement was for the rear of the chassis to fit under the front axle of a horse dray. By the end of 1929 this new tractor was ready for trials and was graced with the name Cob, an ideal stablemate for the Colt!

Despite Karrier's plans for a purpose-built coupling complete with new trailers, the first public demonstration of the Cob in June 1930 (actually undertaken by Karrier themselves) featured an unmodified horse dray with the shafts removed. The coupling gear was a hand winch, which lifted the dray's front axle over the Cob's rear axle. Since there was no braking connection between the two halves of the combination, the road speed was limited to 8 mph.

One very good reason for the use of horse drays on this particular demonstration was that any other users of the new tractor unit were likely to be influenced by the LMS idea on 'lowest costs'. Of course the coupling operation was not up to the ideals of the Karrier design team and they were already working on an updated Cob model along with a modern trailer, complete with a braking system. Whilst the basic 'overlift' gear functioned as intended, its manual operation proved to be slow and laborious. The first demonstration of a railway mechanical horse was made by the LMS Railway on 18th September 1930 and took place at their Maiden Lane Depot in London. The press was informed of this new innovation on 3rd November 1930 and from then on the rest is history.

Above: *The Wolverton coupling had one particular disadvantage in that it required the tractor to have a relatively narrow rear wheel track, in order for the unit to fit between the semi-trailer's landing legs. The landing legs overhung the rear axle of the tractor unit, but the whole of the under-gear had to fit within the maximum 6ft width of the standard LMS trailers of that time. This problem is clearly seen in this picture of a Cob Major and an improved 3¼-ton dray at Wolverton in May 1933. LMS Official*

Below: *A potential problem with the converted horse drays, was that the unsecured loads often slipped and (during sharp braking) could drop into the gap between the tractor and the front of the semi-trailer. By 1936, and with the new Scammell coupling, Cob 791G (pictured in the Spen Valley) is fitted with a 'headboard' - note the 'guard dog' on the bonnet. G. Hawksworth*

At around the same time the Karrier Company arranged a meeting of all the railway Road Motor Engineers to assess the early trials of the Cobs in conjunction with the ex-horse drays. In practice, it seemed that the drays had not performed at all well and the wooden-wheels had rapidly fallen to pieces. The old horse drawn drays were just not up to the job of travelling at 8-10mph, let alone the potential earth shattering 18 mph!

The LMS designers had to go back to the drawing board, obviously looking at more substantial conversions to the horse drays and at the same time seek more money from the Directors to pay for a fleet of suitable new trailers! It was at this point that Karrier revealed their plans for using purpose-built semi-trailers with automatic coupling and trailer braking.

The GWR, SR and LNER were happy with this proposal, but the LMS insisted on returning to the Wolverton coupling, albeit with trailer braking and modifying the drays more by the addition of solid rubber tyres on the rear wheels. Even in the short term this did nothing to alleviate the difficulties faced by the LMS.

At this point it would be appropriate to describe in detail the design of the original Cob, although it may nowadays be better known due to the fact that it was immortalised in a pre-war Dinky Toy model. The tractor featured a very basic cab, and had solid tyres with minimal springing.

Above: *By 1930 both the GWR and the LNER had received prototype Cobs for assessment purposes, here we see an early GWR Cob with the Karrier-style coupling.* Mechanical Horse Club

The Cob was powered by a Jowett 7hp 2-cylinder horizontally-opposed water-cooled petrol engine with a three-speed gearbox and a chain driven 2:1 reduction gear. The reduction gear had a twofold purpose, firstly it allowed the engine to work at its most economic speed, but it also allowed it to be offset in the cab whilst retaining the centre rear differential. The footbrake worked with internally expanding shoes, whilst the handbrake worked with externally contracting bands on the rear brake drums. Despite the small size of engine, the new tractor unit was quite capable of carrying a 3-ton load at 18 mph and could restart on a 1 in 8 gradient fully laden.

A rather less flattering, but perhaps more truthful description of the vehicle is best described in the words of Stanley Sykes who used to work for the Karrier Company. 'Take a half witted draughtsman with a reluctant wife, a hatred of all mankind, especially drivers and recovering from a hangover and there you have it; a channel frame, no springs, 18 inch wheels with solid tyres, the overall appearance of a hospital bed on three castors, and a ride guaranteed to shake the false teeth out of the drivers mouth. A stretch of tramway for the accommodation of the front wheel was a blessing from heaven!'

The engine oil was described as being thick, but others said it was more like weak glue! The gearbox had even thicker oil and the reduction chain case and rear axle used thick gear oil like molten tar. This latter oil, when stored in barrels in the winter needed to be stood on heating pipes before it could be transferred to the greasers. No fan was fitted as the long carburettor induction arms tapered towards the front of the engine.

The LMS ordered 20 Cobs for use with modified drays whilst the GWR and SR purchased 7 and 6 tractors respectively. Just to round off the early part of the Karrier Cob story, we might just add that the Colt 3-wheeled dustcart was given its first public airing at the Institute of Public Cleansing exhibition in the autumn of 1930. (See also the **Nostalgia Road** book, *Municipal Refuse Collection Vehicles*).

The LNER had decided to wait until May 1931 and buy the improved Cob. But soon an even more powerful Cob was to come onto the scene. Known as the 'Cob Major', it looked similar to the original version, but was relieved of the need to squeeze the chassis under horse drays. As a result Karrier were able to replace tiny solid tyres with pneumatics, and then replace the lowly Jowett engine from 1932 with a more powerful water-cooled 4-cylinder 30bhp petrol engine designed by Coventry Climax and built under licence in Huddersfield. A major improvement in ride quality was given with the fitting of telescopic front forks.

This new model was capable of hauling a 4-ton load but it once again had a Karrier-designed coupling gear. The LMS also ordered some Cob Majors, but this time with twin rear wheels and fitted with a Wolverton coupling suitable for use with the modified horse drays. The Karrier Company soon phased out the original Cob and continued to offer the Cob Major until the end of 1932. This model was to re-emerge later in improved form, by which time a rival tractor had arrived on the scene and this will be described in full detail later in this narrative.

The year 1934 saw the new range of Karrier mechanical horses being introduced to the general transport market, but now with a chassis design that was substantially modified from the earlier versions in order to enable heavier loads to be carried. The tractor units came to be marketed as the Cob Major for 4-tons and the Cob Six for 6-ton loads, this latter model being fitted with a 50bhp Triumph engine. The chassis frame was almost diamond shaped in 'plan view', being full width behind the cab, yet narrow between the rear wheels. This chassis was also unusual in that horizontal perforated pressed steel plate was added to the more normal channel section frame.

The engine drove through a normal gearbox into a 'compensating gearbox', which was still an old fashioned chain-driven reduction box. This was used to get the drive from the offset engine and gearbox assembly to the centre of the rear axle. Even so, the cab design was updated quite considerably to give a more modern appeal.

Both larger models made use of the BK coupling mechanism, which Karrier had developed from the original designs by their engineers. These Cobs were supplied to such diverse organisations as Denham Studios to move scenery on long trailers, Peak Freans for moving empty biscuit tins and Spillers for the movement of flour. However, Karrier clearly recognised that its main market was to municipal authorities and the railways, of which the LMS was the most important.

Above: *When Karrier introduced its improved version of the Cob in 1931, the LNER decided to try the vehicle on its cartage services. However it considered that any effective trial would have to be based on having a number of units in service, so it placed a large order for Cob Majors and allocated them to the Leeds area. This was done because this city was relatively close to the Karrier factory in Huddersfield, and warranty and servicing problems could be more readily resolved. This LNER Cob Junior was part of a batch bought in 1936. It was allocated to Kings' Cross Depot, and worked there until it was scrapped in 1946. Note the unusual feature of twin vertical lifting screws to ensure even lifting of the body.* Mechanical Horse Club

Below: *The Karrier Cobs, despite their defects and limitations were to remain effective well into the 1940s. Here we see female fitters servicing a number of Cobs in the LMS garage at Bradford (Croft Street) during 1942.* Courtesy K. Gaunt

By this time the LMS finally succumbed to reason and realised that the use of old horse drays in conjunction with the Wolverton coupling was just not feasible. Karrier might have thought that they had finally won through, but the LMS then began trials with coupling gear made by Scammell Lorries. In due course the LMS settled on the Scammell coupling, and in order for the Huddersfield firm to continue to sell tractors to the railway companies in future they had to offer the Cob with a coupling gear designed to suit that made by their main competitor. In early 1934 the LMS and SR ordered around 200 Cob Major tractors and these were to be fitted with a Scammell design automatic coupling. This version of the coupling became known as the 'J' type as opposed to the AK and BK Karrier designed couplings. The LMS continued to dictate the development. An example of this may be seen by the fact that Cobs built for the LNER, GWR, Southern and South African Railways were simply inspected at the works, but the LMS insisted on a full road test for every individual tractor chassis with a loaded trailer. The LMS (for instance), even specified that all grease nipples should face the same way and be easily accessible.

Back in 1932 the Karrier Company had introduced a new 4-wheel 2-ton load carrying rigid chassis called the Bantam. This was primarily designed as a good quality, small manoeuvrable vehicle ideal for use by municipal authorities for dustcarts and tippers. It was fitted with a Karrier 1122cc 4-cylinder engine and had a four-speed gearbox operating in conjunction with the Cob style chain driven reduction gearbox. The Karrier Company unfortunately became a victim of the financial problems of the early-1930s but was lucky to be taken over by the Rootes group in 1934. At the end of 1935 all the production facilities were moved from Huddersfield to Luton and the Karrier range totally absorbed into the Rootes organisation. The design and development work of all vehicles was thereafter transferred to Luton and this included work on a tractor version of the Bantam 4-wheel rigid model to help increase the models' market share.

Top Left: *This picture shows the Karrier Cob Major demonstrator at Huddersfield early in 1931. The vehicle was initially used by the nearby firm of David Brown Gears, who had been involved in the production, and it was tested between their Park Works and Lockwood Goods Yard.* David Brown Gears

Centre Left: *During the Second World War all road vehicles had to have all outer edges painted white to 'show up' in the blackout. A newly painted Karrier Cob contrasts with the surrounding houses.* Courtesy P. Newman

Bottom Left: *Although the Bantam was selling very well, the 3-wheel market was undoubtedly being dominated by Scammell. As a result the Rootes Group began to look at ways of modernising the image of the Karrier Cob. The final design of Karrier Cob featured a much more modern cab style as exhibited here at Luton's Hoo Station. However, this model never went into full-scale production and the Cob was eventually discontinued.* Courtesy P. Newman.

The MkII version of the Bantam model built at Luton used a Rootes 1944cc engine and a more normal transmission arrangement. The range included a 6ft 0in wheelbase tractor unit with a gross train weight of 8-tons. This tractor featured the Karrier style BK coupling. It retained most of the advantages of the Cob except for a certain loss of ultimate manoeuvrability. Yet this little 4-wheeler offered greater stability than the Cob by having a wheel at each corner, and as such was partly responsible for the relative decline in Cob sales after 1936. Soon the more direct transmission system and the BK coupling of the Bantam was transferred to an updated Cob range.

These latest Cobs made use of a more normal chassis design and the BK coupling consisted of two inclined ramps on the rear of the tractor chassis, these engaged with rollers on the trailer turntable underside and also included automatic linkage of the trailer braking system. These new Cobs were marketed with two alternative couplings: the BK based on the original Karrier principles and the J type which was based on the rival Scammell design and thus fully compatible with Scammell trailers.

The 1936 Rootes Group 3-wheel and 4-wheel tractor range was:

Model	Payload	Engine	BK Type	J Type
Colt	2 tons	Rootes 4-cyl 40bhp.	-	-
Cob Junior	4 tons	Rootes 4-cyl 40bhp	Yes	Yes
Cob Senior	6 tons	Rootes 6-cyl 70bhp.	Yes	Yes
Bantam	2/4 tons	Rootes 4-cyl 40bhp	Yes	No

Both industry and the railways readily accepted this new range, and these new Cobs were altogether a much better model than their predecessors had been. The cab was much larger, initially coach built, but soon made from pressed steel, though the LMS were in a position to manufacture their own cabs. Business was good, and in 1936 the railway companies placed orders for over 200 Cob Juniors fitted with the Scammell based J type coupling.

Top Right: *This early Karrier Bantam Mk.1 tractor unit, fitted with a BK-type coupling and trailer, is being backed into a factory loading bay in an 'arranged' publicity shot. The low-built cab on the Bantam features easy access from both sides, and is fitted with a single headlamp, one windscreen wiper and an attractive chrome radiator. Karrier Motors, courtesy Mechanical Horse Club.*

Centre Right: *Another view of a Bantam, employed by the firm of J. Lyons & Co. This firm started out as a tobacconists, and soon moved into supplying the hotel trade. In due course they extended their interests into confectionery supplies and the operation of the famous 'Corner House' restaurants. They also became well known for their cakes, beverages, and ice cream, and in the delivery of these products they employed a large number of mechanical horses. A. Ingram*

Bottom Right: *The Bantam continued to be a firm favourite with many operators, and this tractor was purchased by the Eastern Region of BR in the summer of 1949. It is coupled with a mobile ticket office for the sale of cheap summer excursion tickets. British Railways*

Above: *Not all Karrier 3-wheelers were articulated and here we see a rigid model. This Colt was a hand-operated tipper used by the coal merchants Shaws of Milnsbridge near Huddersfield. As this company operated a large fleet of horse-drawn coal wagons, it was natural they would try mechanisation when offered to them for evaluation by Karrier who were based 3 miles away. It was a two-way arrangement, and Karrier extensively used this picture in their publicity material.* Karrier Motors Courtesy K. Millett.

Below: *Not all the articulated railway lorries were mechanical horses and here we see Bedford WHG tractor unit being used to move a trailer with a Mobile Canteen in July 1942 These canteens were developed during World War II in order to sustain permanent way workers employed on emergency track repairs (after air raids etc.), at a time when lines had to be returned to operation inside 24 hours.* LNER Official

These models continued in production until the start of World War II, although the Rootes Group bowed to the inevitable pressure from the transport industry and introduced the J type (Scammell compatible) coupling to the Bantam from 1938. Another major step forward was the introduction of servo-assisted Bendix brakes to all the tractor rear axles from 1937.

The fitting of the Triumph 6-cylinder engine to the Cob 6 was not completely trouble free. The engine had been designed for use with twin carburettors, but on the Cob the requirement was for a single carburettor and a new manifold. This led to many problems with number 1 and 6 cylinders either running weak or rich. When the Cob 6 was replaced by the Cob Senior the engine used was a Humber 6-cylinder side valve, which did away with the induction problems of the earlier engine.

Despite the seemingly glowing future for Rootes' small tractor units, the Ministry of Supply decreed from the outbreak of war that the company's tractor units were to be phased out of production. The market for small-articulated units being catered for by Scammell Lorries with their own mechanical horses and the Bedford Scammell OSS (later wartime OXC) models. Instead the Rootes group were to produce a number of military vehicles for the war effort. The final delivery of Cob Juniors for the railway companies was in 1940.

When peace returned in 1945 the Bantam tractor was again made available, and the following year saw the resumption of production of the 3-wheelers, but in redesigned form with an even more up to date cab. In the higher weight category the Rootes Group introduced the Commer Q4 Superpoise 4-wheel 6- to 8-ton tractor to compete with the all-conquering Bedford OSS tractor.

Both of these models featured in the railway company purchase lists in rigid and tractor format. When the railway companies got round to deciding which of the competing 3-wheel tractor units they should order, the Scammell company won most of the orders. The LNER actually went as far as running comparative trials between a Cob Junior and a Bantam. The 4-wheeler seemed to receive approval, and the Bantam joined the Scammell Mechanical Horse to become the LNER's standard articulated delivery vehicles in the future.

Over at the LMS at least one post- war Cob Junior was purchased for assessment, but orders were not forthcoming, and the Cob was dropped from the Rootes group line up after 1949. As a postscript to the involvement of the Karrier company with the railways, large orders were placed for Bantams in the 1960s and many of these remained in operation until the demise of the small articulated vehicles.

As a final comment on the Karrier group 3-wheelers, during the mid- to late-1930s, the Rootes Group advertised a Tilling Stevens battery electric tractor for $2^{1}/_{4}$-ton payloads. This vehicle was based on a normal Cob chassis and made use of Tilling Stevens' electrical know-how. Actual sales volumes remain a mystery though an ex-employee recalls that only three or four were ever built, but none seem to have been sold and they finished their days as shunters at the Maidstone factory where the Tilling Stevens (and later, Vulcan) commercials were built. The history of these 3-wheelers is hoped to be covered in a future Nostalgia Road book examining the history of battery-electric vehicles.

CHAPTER 3. THE SCAMMELL MECHANICAL HORSE

Although the Karrier Cob became the first mechanical horse, an upstart whose origins go back to early 1931 soon surpassed it. In that year the LNER decided to sponsor an alternative vehicle to the offering from Huddersfield. The LNER did not wish to develop mechanical horses themselves, but they did establish a basic specification for such a beast. An agent was then engaged to find a manufacturer willing to undertake the necessary development.

The agent by chance met an engineer from the Napier Company who were famous for designing and building aero engines. At that time Napier were looking for work as a result of both the general depression and the fact that re-armament was not then being considered in Britain.

The outcome of the meeting was that the Napier Company agreed to develop a 3-wheeled tractor and articulated trailer to replace the horse on railway 'town cartage' duties. The company got as far as building one or two prototypes that met with LNER approval, and arrangements were put in hand for a limited production run. However, Napier's decided not to continue with the project, so the agent then approached Scammell Lorries who agreed to take over the development of the 'mechanical horse'.

Above: *This is one of the earliest Scammell Mechanical Horses supplied to the LMS railway and used for experiments with the Wolverton coupling. These early 'horses featured a separate wing for the front wheel, a half door and a cut away 'B' pillar. Most of the railway 'horses featured the deep cowl and vertical windscreen as seen in this photo. The trailer No.3394 is based on a strengthened horse-drawn design and the rods/cables under the chassis operate the rear brakes. The rear trailer springs were also mounted on a wooden subframe, but this was a poor design feature for a motor vehicle. This particular Mechanical Horse, seen near Wolverton in May 1933, was taking part in the evaluation trials, and was photographed so that comparative pictures could be viewed by senior management. The tractor unit is registered JH 4713, but the trailer carries a set of trade plates (024 AR) that were allocated to the LMS.* LMS Official

All of the Napier prototypes, and the tooling and manufacturing rights were passed to Scammell. The chief designer at Scammell, a Mr. O. D. North acknowledged the innovative nature of the Napier design, but felt that certain fundamental changes would enhance the commercial viability of the vehicle. These added features were to become the very key to the success over the Karrier Cob.

17

Above: *A prototype mechanical horse built by Napier, painted in LMS colours and probably fitted with a version of the Wolverton coupling. The fundamental design of the Mechanical Horse can be seen, especially in the cab, yet it still has a vaguely familiar look of the Karrier Cob. Note the fact that it rides on Goodyear tyres.*

Below: *This 3-ton Mechanical Horse, is an early example of the type employed by the LNER and it entered service at Nottingham Goods Station on 8th November 1933. The picture shows the process of road-rail interchange, as 6 tierces (barrels) of tobacco are loaded by means on an overhead 'Goliath' crane on to the semi trailer. These containers weigh nearly half a ton each, and the width extends well outside the platform. One wonders how stable such a load would be to drive, but when this picture was taken in February 1943 overloading was commonplace due to the many war-time transport difficulties.* LNER Official

The Scammell company had origins in the horse carriage trade as wheelwrights and waggon builders. They had originally been based in Spitalfields in East London as George Scammell and later traded as G. Scammell & Nephew Ltd. The company had moved out to Watford in Hertfordshire, to allow themselves room to develop the articulated 6-wheeler, and in 1922 it changed its name to Scammell Lorries Ltd.

Whilst keeping to the mainstream of building heavier trucks by 1932, their amazingly talented chief designer had already designed some very advanced vehicles. These included the Auto-Van and earlier the North-Lucas car which although unsuccessful were noted as very advanced for their time. The North-Lucas car had a 5-cylinder side valve 1460cc air-cooled radial engine lying flat above the rear axle. The streamlined bodywork was built to function also as the chassis, and this was a very early form of monocoque construction. North's most spectacular success to date had been the Scammell Pioneer 6-wheeler built for colonial and eventually military use, but numerous features of the car were to be found on later North/Scammell designs.

The articulated coupling designed by the Napier team had close similarities to the Wolverton coupling, but Scammell realised that it could be improved. The railway company had specified the need for the coupling to work with loaded or empty trailers, to work on any road surface (generally the setts or cobbles to be found in railway yards), at any reasonable angle between tractor and trailer and to be the ultimate in simplicity. In fact they wanted the coupling to work automatically!

A coupling to suit the criteria was designed by Mr. North, and was in concept quite simple, though very ingenious in design and engineering terms. This was then fitted to a Napier 3-wheeled chassis modified by Scammell. It must be noted that there had been earlier versions of the automatic coupling, in one case dating back to 1906 when the German company Hansa Automobil had introduced a skate type coupling with a separate retractable landing leg. Somewhat later, in 1920, the Belgian Minerva Company had introduced their 'Auto Traction' 4-wheel tractor and semi trailer with a large, heavy duty, coupling gear. However, none of the earlier designs were able to meet the exacting needs of the LMS!

On the Scammell redesign of the original Napier Mechanical Horse, the rear chassis cross-member was omitted completely and two narrow, rather bent looking, pressed steel ramps were mounted on the appropriately shaped rear chassis frames. The front of the ramps were joined by a massive box section cross-member on which was mounted the locking device. On the early trailers this lock was a single pair of claws, but this was soon modified to incorporate two pairs of claws which engaged with two pairs of small rollers mounted on the underside of the trailer's turntable.

Fitted to the front of the ramp were spring-loaded buffers and 'C' shaped retaining hooks, which were designed to prevent lateral and vertical movement of the trailer when coupled. The job of the buffers was to 'load' the coupling hooks and ensure that the trailer was securely locked to the unit. On the trailer itself the coupling components consisted of a forged beam that pivoted under the turntable, and this enabled the trailer chassis to move in relation to the unit.

At the end of this beam were two flanged wheels. Under the forged beam was a series of paired, hinged metal struts that made up the undercarriage and this assembly ran on two large steel jockey wheels.

To couple the unit and trailer together all the driver had to do was to reverse his Mechanical Horse towards the trailer. As the tip of the ramps engaged with the flanged wheels, and the driver continued reversing, the small flanged wheels travelled up the ramp lifting the jockey wheels off the ground. As the driver reversed even further, a spring-loaded catch forced the undercarriage to fold up (or retract) backwards thereby giving increased ground clearance. Simultaneously the claws on the tractor engaged with the rollers mounted under the forged beam giving a positive connection. At the same time the brake and lights were also automatically connected.

The trailers brakes were mechanically operated by a centrally mounted slipper pad on the tractor's coupling gear making direct contact with various bell cranks and levers operating through the central turntable and then a cable linkage to the rear axle of the trailer. The lighting connection consisted of direct contact between two brass plates mounted on both parts of the combination.

The braking system was so arranged that the trailer brakes came on fractionally before the tractor unit's brakes to help the whole combination stop in a straight line. As far as the driver was concerned he had only to release the trailer's mechanical handbrake and move the registration plate and rear light (lights from the 1950s) from the tractor unit to the rear of the trailer. There was definitely no need for the driver to line up the tractor and trailer accurately; the coupling did the work for him. Unlike today there were no landing legs to wind up, nor any electrical or air Suzies to connect.

One of the first pre-production prototypes of the Scammell Mechanical Horse was exhibited at the Scottish Motor Show late in 1932, and was then the subject of a press release in the trade newspaper *Motor Transport* on 5th November. A sales advertisement appeared in the trade press in the spring of 1933 announcing that Scammell's would 'shortly be in a position to commence deliveries' and that the company was still looking for agencies to sell the vehicle in certain areas. On 3rd June 1933 *Motor Transport* devoted a whole page article to the new mechanical horses and noted that many modifications had been made to the vehicles in the months since the Scottish Show.

On demonstration at Kings Langley near Watford the *Motor Transport* journalist found that a loaded 3-ton 'horse could climb a steady gradient of 1 in 7½. It could stop and start easily on the same gradient and also turn round on the same hill, which was 18 feet wide, and would also couple and uncouple on the same gradient.

The company had initially intended the vehicle to be built in three capacities. There were to be 3-ton and 5-ton models using the smaller engine and a 6-tonner with the larger engine, but Scammell's soon dropped the potentially under-powered 5-tonner. The vehicles were built to the same basic design as the Karrier Cob, but were a little more sophisticated than its competitor. Once the trade had been made aware of the new vehicle it was finally presented to the public on 7th September 1933.

Above: *Here we show a Southern Railway 3-ton Mechanical Horse demonstrating the workings of the automatic coupling outside the Scammell works. The upper picture shows the trailer coupling travelling up the ramps as the 'horse reverses, very soon afterwards the undercarriage would retract to give adequate ground clearance.*

Below: *Taken on the same day, this photograph shows how the driver could 'nudge' the coupling round if the tractor approaches from the wrong angle. The photograph also displays the 'bent steel ramps'. Note that the trailer's handbrake is firmly in the 'on' position, just under the headboard.*

To the outsider all the production Scammell 3-wheelers must have looked alike, certainly they all used water-cooled engines, but of course there were many differences. The 3-ton model had a Scammell 10hp 1125cc petrol engine and large section 8.25x10 pneumatic tyres all round, whilst its larger brother could boast a 15hp 2043cc engine, with much larger 10.50 x 13 tyres at the rear. The two capacities of vehicle had almost identical patterns of coupling gear for 3- or 6-ton loads, but of totally different dimensions and totally incompatible with each other.

Both engines used a single plate clutch and a David Brown constant mesh four-speed gearbox driving a spur and bevel double reduction rear axle. A variety of different final drive ratios were made available and it was an easy job to alter the ratio by changing the spur gears. With the single front wheel able to rotate through 180 degrees, the solo vehicle was able to turn in less than its own length. The front suspension made use of coil springs with adjustable friction dampers, with the rear axle being fitted with leaf springs.

Above: *The major users of the Mechanical Horse, the railways, did not find diesel engines a viable option. Industrial users found much better use for models like this Scammell-Perkins diesel with a 12-ton grain hopper in Belfast.* Mechanical Horse Club

The whole concept was remarkably simple and the coupling proved virtually foolproof and totally satisfactory to the LNER who had instigated this particular design. Their very first order was placed for 80 tractors and over 113 trailers to work principally at Farringdon Street Depot in London. By late-1933 more orders for Mechanical Horses and their associated trailers began arriving at the Watford factory situated in Tolpits Lane. (Tolpits is probably a derivation of an earlier Two Pits Lane). After the initial batch for the LNER, orders were placed by the GWR. Then in July the instigators of the concept, the LMS Railway, ate humble pie and purchased a batch of Scammell Mechanical Horses to complement their existing fleet of Cobs.

Top Right: *We now present another picture of interest for Irish readers, with this view of a Great North Of Ireland Railway 6-ton Mechanical Horse. Painted in the livery of Inglis Quality Bread, the railway ownership is donated by the small oval cast number plate below the window. Note the demountable containers on the trailer.*

Centre Right: *Engaged on rather more prestigious delivery work, this 1947 3-ton MH is leaving the Knightsbridge depot of the Harrods department store with a container supplied by the Southern Railway.*

Bottom Right: *The 'frameless-tank' trailers were widely employed in the transport of all types of bulk fluid, including Molasses Here we see a 6-ton tractor photographed outside Watford Isolation Hospital in the 1930s.* All Mechanical Horse Club

As we have shown, the success of the Scammell coupling was so resounding that Karrier, the real originator of the idea, had to start offering their own version of the Scammell coupling in order to keep receiving business from the railway companies. In order to get round the patents, the Karrier coupling differed from the Scammell design by using positively sprung 'C' shaped hooks that fitted over the small flanged wheels so as to retain the trailer coupling in position. On the Scammell version it was the central jaws that retained the trailer. Despite the introduction of the Scammell models the Karrier Cob still continued to sell in small numbers, not just to the railway companies, but to many manufacturers and local merchants who appreciated the lower acquisition price and the competitive running costs.

By 1938 the LMS were commenting that 'the mechanical horse within its proper capacity and radius of action is the cheapest form of motor vehicle to run. It's operating advantages are greatest when it is possible to operate a shuttle service with two or even more trailers and, in addition a number of different trailers for carrying varying and specialised loads which might not be working full time. The remarkable freedom to manoeuvre possessed by the mechanical horse also makes it of great use in congested areas, and it is true to say that the mechanisation of certain stations built years ago when only horse traffic was envisaged would have been impossible without it'.

Once the basic design of a 3-wheeler tractor and its attendant trailers was settled (and production was under way for railway companies and their cartage agents), then Scammell's set about widening the market for this unique concept. The main marketing ploy hinged around the ultimate versatility of the vehicles; for not only could they replace the four legged horse (and avoid the necessity of looking after them 365 days per year), but they could also give major increases in productivity.

A single Mechanical Horse could carry up to a 6-ton payload (a figure later increased to 15-tons for internal use). Whilst one trailer was being loaded another trailer could be out on delivery and a third could be discharging its load and all of these trailers could be handled by one tractor unit. In addition a wide variety of alternative trailer bodies or styles were made available. The main question was, whom should the salesman direct his effort towards?

At the time of the Mechanical Horses' introduction the whole country had been plunged into the era of the Great Depression, so there was not a great deal of money about. However, certain markets could afford to purchase new vehicles especially if these new vehicles could offer real value for money and substantially reduce operating costs. Who were these potential customers? Well of course they included brewers, gas manufacturing companies, electricity companies, municipal authorities, dairies, coal merchants and retailing chains all of whom could offset the effects of the Depression by reducing the operating costs incurred in servicing their guaranteed markets. What all these operators had in common were urban operations with a need to both replace horses and exchange trailers on a very regular basis! Some operators' names taken at random from the order book include the brewers Fremlins, Courage and Chesters, coal merchant Charringtons, Gartons Glucose, United Molasses, Shell Mex and BP as well as a number of co-operative societies and the General Post Office. Perhaps the most prestigious name amongst the early operators was Harrods the up-market department store!

Dropside, flat platforms, tankers, brewers' drays and tippers were regularly despatched from the Watford factory and covered vans later became fairly common purchases for the railway companies. Among the more specialised were some twin axle heavy-duty trailers used by Liverpool Cartage and within large factories.

One rather novel feature on the earlier 'horses which was carried over from the Cob, was the mounting of the sidelights at roof level on adjustable brackets which allowed the lights to be swung out to indicate the overall width of the trailer. Incidentally the only easy way to date a Mechanical Horse apart from the registration, is by the positioning of the headlamp. The earliest models had it mounted flush with the cowl about half way up the nearside front of the vehicle. By about 1936 the lamp was being fitted externally on the nearside of the front wheel and post war versions had the lamp fitted to the offside of the front wheel.

Top Left: *In addition to the railways, the biggest customers for the Mechanical Horse were the many local authorities in Britain. Individual sales may have not been large, some rural district councils would only buy one or two tractor units, but collectively the potential was enormous. Here we see a Scammell demonstrator with a 'moving floor' compaction system in its semi-trailer body.* Derek Andrews

Centre Left: *By 1939 over 60 municipalities had 'revolutionised' their transport with the introduction of vehicles including street washers, gully emptiers, bin carriers and refuse collectors based on the Mechanical Horse. This 3-ton model, pictured during a demonstration, has a rather more esoteric trailer in the form of a Johnston-Scammell road sweeper.* Mechanical Horse Club

Bottom Left:*The City of Glasgow, were always innovators in refuse collection methods. They bought several 3-ton tractors, and equipped them with different types of trailer, including this curtained side-loader with 4-bays and a crew compartment.* Derek Andrews

The cab styles varied quite considerably, but the more discerning customers could expect doors, a sloping windscreen and shallower cowl. If you were a municipal customer then generally a slightly deeper cab was supplied, thus giving a greater internal length. The only apparent reason for this being that a passenger could be carried in a little more comfort. In the basic Mechanical Horse the engine was offset to the left, that meant that the passenger seat was perched above the engine and the passenger's feet could not touch the floor. On the bumpy roads of the day, if he wished to steady himself, the passenger could only lean forward and if he did he was likely to burn his hand on the hot radiator! In municipal use a second man was often necessary and his comfort was presumably quite important so the seat was set lower and further back.

Internally the vehicle remained very basic, both seats and pedals were non-adjustable. The instrumentation was minimal to say the least with just an ammeter and a Geeson speed indicator that illuminated above a pre-set speed, which was about 18mph. A mileage recorder was available and fitted onto the side of the differential casing, but there was never the opportunity to have the mileage recorded within the cab. The fuel tank was mounted above the driver's knees with an external filler cap; on the other hand the radiator had its filler inside the cab. Needless to say there were many occasions when the incorrect fluid entered the wrong filler cap much to the consternation of the driver and fitters.

To the end of the Mechanical Horse's production life it retained a petrol engine as standard, although a Perkins diesel was available as an option from August 1937 onwards. The petrol version never had a starter motor, and hand cranking was always the order of the day. The railway horses had a windscreen wiper the size of a pencil and when it rained the vision was limited to an area of about six inches across. When the more basic 'horses came to be fitted with doors the lowest cost option was chosen in the form of door latches like those found on a garden gate. If the driver went over a rough road he had to hold the door to stop it flying open. However, by the mid-1940s the horse was looking a bit long in the tooth and needed to be put out to grass!

Top Right: *The railways usually bought the cheapest possible cab with half height canvas sheets in place of doors, the horizontally split windscreen was mounted vertically. Here two contrasting 'preserved' Scammells are seen on display at York Station in August 1998.* Alan Earnshaw (courtesy Railtrack plc)

Centre Right: *With the engine being mounted fairly high in the chassis and offset to the left, the tractor had an embarrassing tendency to 'fall over' on sharp right hand turns, like this LMS unit at Dudley. In a similar incident in Portsmouth the front wheel of a tractor unit 'slipped' on some droppings left by one of its four footed cousins.* The Office of The Chief Constable, Dudley

Bottom Right: *Thousands of 'horses saw 'military service', and many were later sold to British Railways or industrial users. This one (seen in London) may have been bought by J. Nall of Bolton who had been cartage agents for the LMS.* P. Newman

Above: *A 1933 Commer 4-ton tractor unit with a Brockhouse 'Kwikfiks' coupling and trailer used by Revo Electric for delivering electric cookers in September 1934.* Mechanical Horse Club

CHAPTER 4. PASTURES NEW

Although designed with local delivery use in mind, the 6-ton coupling gear gradually came to the notice of the road hauliers. By converting a rigid vehicle to an articulated combination a useful doubling of payload could be gained for less than the cost of buying two rigid vehicles. During the 1930s, a number of firms began offering articulated conversions to new 4-wheeled short wheelbase commercial vehicle chassis. Most of these early conversions were based on variations of the fifth wheel introduced on the Knox tractor 20 years earlier. Many of the earlier conversions featured various Bedford models due to their inherent, inbuilt capacity to be overloaded. The best known of all the articulated converters was the firm of Carrimore Six Wheelers of Finchley, who began their conversion of Bedford chassis in 1935. These conversions proved that articulation could be successfully applied to mass-produced trucks as well as to the higher priced/higher quality models.

Other well-known names involved with early-articulated conversions include: - Taskers of Andover, The Truck & Tractor Appliance Co. of Trafford Park, Manchester (whose trailer was called the Dragon), Eagle of Warwick, Flexicon from Hendon in North London and G. Scammell & Nephew of Spitalfields.

These companies were all amongst the leaders in this particular market. The majority of these articulated combinations simply took advantage of the additional payload that could be gained rather than the possibility of using different trailers. The Dragon trailer was featured quite widely in the press releases of the time (mid-1930s) and these stated that a Thornycroft truck of 2-ton capacity could legally carry a 3½-ton payload. It also propounded that running costs came to only 1d (½p) per mile and that it took only a minute to uncouple the trailer.

continues on page 29

Above: *Here we see two 3-ton Mechanical Horses, superbly restored in the LNER livery, at the National Railway Museum's Railways & Roads event in August 1998. Apart from the modern road markings in the picture, this could easily have been taken any time during the 1930s or '40s. The right hand tractor demonstrates the very basic accommodation for the passenger and the lack of doors in the earliest models.* Alan Earnshaw

Right: *The Grimsby Ice Company converted most of its petrol engined Mechanical Horses to battery electric power during the fifties. This shot shows fleet number two, JV 9054, delivering barrels of ice to the fish merchants Frank Hool (Grimsby) who were based at 50, North End Pontoon, Fish Docks.*

Above: *The Sheffield steel industry was a major user of Scammell 3-wheelers, as these versatile vehicles could get into the small workshops around the city. In the cramped area where the 'Little Misters' operated their artisan workshops, the Scarabs and Mechanical Horses moved thousands of pieces of cutlery. Steel springs would be taken from the many wireworks for tempering, and even large billets would be seen on the back of an auto-coupling trailer. One of the final users was the Firth Brown Company, and this 3-tonner 143 DWB (Fleet No. 70) dating from 1962 is shown at work in the firm's Atlas Works in 1980 - it has survived into preservation.*

Left: *A complete contrast to industrial Sheffield, was the historic city of Beverley in East Yorkshire, but it also saw industrial use of Scarabs. Here (in 1982) a late model 6-ton Scarab is moving raw materials from the BTP Cocker Chemicals warehouse on Beverley Beck to their main works. Note the basic signwriting on the doors!*

Above: *The Great Western Railway designed a standard 'Safety Cab' to fit on many of the chassis ordered by the company, including Mechanical Horses of various types. This policy was continued into British Railways days, and we show an example of it fitted to a 1949 Thornycroft Nippy articulated tractor. The vehicle, seen at the National Railway Museum in 1998 has been restored in BR's Eastern Region livery, who were the final user of the vehicle after it was transferred from the Western Region.* Alan Earnshaw

Right: *By the mid-1960s the days of the 3-wheel tractor unit were rapidly diminishing, and of the 4-wheelers the Karrier Bantam was becoming a little dated. This opened the door for Ford when it introduced its D series in the mid-1960s, and the articulated tractor became a very popular vehicle with National Carriers. This 1978 model, pictured in Grimsby in November 1981, shows an auto trailer with a side-loading door on the van trailer.*

Above: *The Imperial Chemical Company and its transport contractors used automatic coupling vehicles over a long period, and one of the final purchases was this Scottish built Leyland Chieftain. Dating from 1981, JDC 302W is seen at the Wilton plant on Teesside, complete with an elliptical tank carrying Gas Oil. By this time the regulations required additional secondary braking facilities, resulting in the need for the driver to couple air hoses to the tank trailer.*

Left: *Like ICI, the General Post Office had long been users of the automatic coupling system and we will cover their vehicles in our forthcoming book* Royal Mail Vehicles of the 1950s and '60s. *In the late-1960s and early-1970s they began purchasing the Ford D series tractor unit. Many of these lasted quite a while, as for example Hull, where a fleet of van trailers were retained for transporting mail between the station and the sorting office and also for parcel delivery work. Here WAT 837J is seen with Hull Only Trailer No.4 in 1978.*

Despite the success of the Scammell automatic coupling on the small 3-wheelers, it took almost five years for the concept to be transferred to the larger 4-wheel vehicles. Once again it seems as though it was the LMS Railway that brought the concept to fruition. They combined a short wheelbase Dennis 40/45cwt chassis/cab (often described as flying pigs due to their long bonnet and set back rear axle) with the 6-ton MH coupling gear in early 1938. Most of the earliest Dennis chassis came to be fitted with the 'bent steel' type of ramps which looked as if they had been reversed hard into a brick wall, but all future conversions came to be fitted with much stronger cast steel ramps. This order for Dennis vehicles was soon followed by orders for Thornycroft Nippy 3-ton chassis converted with the 6-ton automatic coupling, with the LMS and GWR both acquiring examples.

However, it was not until the Bedford Company took the Scammell coupling concept to heart that the market for Scammell automatic couplings for haulage use really began to grow. At the Scottish Motor Show in the autumn of 1938 a matched Bedford-Scammell combination was displayed and on 3rd February 1939 the concept was officially launched with combinations for 6- to 8-ton loads available direct from Bedford dealers. For 6-ton loads the WHG chassis was utilised while the 8-tonner relied on the heavier duty WTH chassis. The most important item to note about the link between Scammell and Bedford was that the unit and trailer could be ordered as a complete package from the Bedford dealer. The cost of the basic Bedford tractor unit was £280 when they were officially announced in the spring of 1939.

The tractor was built to the correct specification to suit the Scammell coupling gear, by having modified rear chassis and springs to fit under the Scammell coupling, as well as different rear axle ratios and of course uprated brakes. The Bedford dealer could handle any warranty problems on either truck or coupling. The close working relationship between Bedford and Scammell was in complete contrast to problems that could arise with other coupling and trailer manufacturers, with each blaming the other when warranty faults arose.

Top Right: *This early Bedford-Scammell 5-ton WTH tractor unit was owned by Hopping Bros. Timber Merchants of Whetstone, London. The unit ran a regular service from Surrey Commercial Docks to either Whetsone or the firm's stockyard in Kent, as well as deliveries to builders' merchants or construction sites. It averaged 25,000 miles a year and remained in service for over 10 years.* Vauxhall Motors

Centre Right: *When the BBC began operating its television services, a decision was made to employ the Scammell coupling system so that a variety of special trailers (from generators to outside broadcast studios) could be used with a limited number of OSS tractors. Even so, in the first five years Bedford supplied no less than 80 new tractor units to the Corporation.* Scammell Lorries Courtesy K. Upson.

Bottom Right: *A batch of OSS tractor units were supplied to London Transport in 1947 for use with mobile canteen semi-trailers, some of which were built on ex-WD low-loaders.* Mechanical Horse Club

One important modification was to the braking system with all the 4-wheel tractor units gaining power operation of the mechanical trailer brakes. This was achieved through a vacuum cylinder mounted on the tractor that operated the slipper, which connected to the trailer's foundation brakes. Much later the uncoupling mechanism became power-operated too. The variety of bodies that came to be fitted to the trailers was as wide as those listed above for the 3-wheelers. However, amongst the most interesting regular production offerings were the frameless tankers. Built exactly as the name states the tank itself acted as the chassis frame and the coupling gear and axles were mounted directly on the tank shell. This gave quite a weight saving over a conventional articulated tanker and became very popular with the petrol companies. The tank shells generally would have been supplied to Scammells by outside contractors like Butterfields or Thompsons (Bilston) Ltd.

Looking back it seems amazing that a normal 3- to 4-ton payload vehicle such as a Bedford O type, Commer Superpoise or a Thornycroft Nippy or even a Dennis 40/45cwt chassis could be converted to haul a 6-ton payload or more. This was managed by the simple expedient of adding a coupling gear, changing carburettor jets, possibly uprating the brakes and maybe altering the rear axle ratio. It certainly would not happen today under EC regulations. One big advantage of articulated trailers over drawbar trailers was that no second man was needed in the cab to work the trailer brakes.

Top Left: *An early post-war Dennis Horla demonstrator poses for the camera during a publicity session at the Scammell works. The Horla was the tractor version of the highly popular Dennis Pax and in this instance was fitted with a Dennis petrol engine.*

Centre Left: *Here we see the Scammell Automatic Coupling as fitted to a Thornycroft Nippy tractor unit. Shown clearly are two rods, the nearest operates the trailer brakes through the coupling gear, whilst the further one uncouples the trailer by depressing the hooks shown in the top centre of the photograph.*

Bottom Left: *One of many Dennis Horla tractor units operated by the Whitbread brewery company, complete with a distinctive 40-barrel (1,440 gallon) frameless tank trailer built by Thompsons of Bilston.*

Top Right: *This British Railways (Western Region) 3-ton load carrier is quite a rare beast, even more so as the picture shows one of those built with twin rear wheels to give a low loading height. The cab was built at BR Swindon works and is based on the pre-war 'Safety Cab' design that featured a sliding door on the driver's side. A number of these were introduced to work in low entry warehouses in the London, Birmingham and Bristol areas, but the allocation details are, to say the least, very confusing. More information on these twin wheel and single wheel BR rigids is urgently sought.* British Railways Western Region

CHAPTER 5. MODIFIED HORSES

One other small market also open to Scammells was for 3-wheel rigid load carriers with a carrying capacity of up to 3-tons. Once again the Karrier Company with their Colt model had pioneered this particular market, although it always appeared very under-engineered compared with its Scammell counterpart. This was especially true of one of the demonstrator Cobs with a covered refuse body. The cab roof was integral with the body so that when the body tipped, the cab was uncovered and of course it always seemed to rain when tipping took place.

However, what Scammell did was to combine the engineering of the 6-ton Mechanical Horse with a longer, straight chassis frame and offer it as a 3-ton load carrier. Although not widely popular it did find many customers, both as a small municipal dustcart and as a dray for brewery companies. The LNER certainly bought a number for use in goods transhipment sheds and railway owned markets. This model was sometimes marketed as 'The Trivan' and later some GWR articulated mechanical horses were converted into rigid load carriers.

Although none of these rigids entered preservation, one ex-RAF/Grimsby Ice Company 6-ton tractor unit has been rebuilt as a load carrier and is displayed as a 'Benskin's Brewery' dray.

Above: *Snow clearance in Leeds with one of the City Councils many Mechanical Horses. In this instance a rigid version (GUB 602) is shown working as a snowplough in the company of a Case tractor. Many authorities used Mechanical Horses on gritting work, normally employing trailers ordinarily used in refuse collection or park department duties.*

Below: *Here we see LMS Fleet number 1H probably prior to delivery to the railway company. This was their prototype lightweight Mechanical Horse, which weighed a mere 16cwt (800 kg). It was a very crude design to look at, but featured many advanced mechanical components that were to be used in a later model.*

One well-documented fleet of rigids was that owned by the Scottish Co-operative Wholesale Society. The society had purchased some ex-Ministry MH's, and then converted them to 3-wheel load carriers for use as milk floats. The main point of interest in these conversions was the use of diesel engines that came to be fitted low in the chassis behind the cab rather than beside the driver.

Other conversions of interest include a 6-ton tractor unit into a basic fork lift truck, which was used in Lincolnshire. In the Midlands, one tractor unit was converted for use as a site tipper, and thereafter employed in the movement of slag at International Alloys in Sutton Coldfield. It was recorded as carrying more than 100 tons of slag a week over a three year period and the only alteration had been to uprate the rear tyres to twin 7.50-20 and to fit a tipping gear. This same company also altered another 'horse to a works fire engine.

Actually Scammell offered a fire engine variant as a regular production option, though very few came to be built and the only large batch was sold to the RAF. Obviously Scammell's own works fire engine was naturally a Mechanical Horse but in its later years this appliance usually needed a tow around the works before it would start!

During the early lifetime of the Scammell Mechanical Horse, attempts were made to introduce a lower priced model that would carry a 30cwt load, that is half the carrying capacity of the 3-ton 'horse. Probably instigated by the LMS and LNER and designed at Scammells it was not destined to be a success and was probably more of a design project than a production certainty. The early prototypes proved unreliable and wartime conditions had to some extent obviated the need for a lightweight horse. Power was supplied by an air-cooled 60 degrees, V twin engine situated approximately amidships. The engine had the lowly capacity of 832cc and developed just 15bhp at 3000 rpm.

The engine, clutch, three-speed gearbox and rear axle were constructed in one unit, and were anchored to the front of the chassis frame by a large rubber bush. The rear suspension was certainly very advanced for the time (1937), using steel coil springs complete with hydraulic shock absorbers, the whole mechanical units being located at the rear by a transverse link fitted with rubber bushes. All the driving and braking torque was transmitted through the engine, gearbox and axle unit to the front anchorage. This whole unit was designed to be readily detachable for maintenance, and as it was situated behind the cab, it gave the driver easy access into the cab from either side. The steering gear was similar to that of its larger brother, but featured a rubber suspension spring rather than the coil spring that sufficed for the 3- and 6-ton models.

The LNER prototype was registered EGT 918; it commenced work at King's Cross in October 1937 and was withdrawn from Tynemouth in 1948. Despite its clever design features it was only produced in small numbers, but a number of the innovative design features found themselves in a totally different vehicle after the war.

From about 1938 a major new customer appeared and was soon placing large orders, the customer was the Government and the tractors and trailers were soon in use in the many military bases, airfields and ordnance stores that were springing up across the country.

CHAPTER 6. TRUCKS AND TRAILERS

Excessive demand for Scammell lorries and trailers early in the war meant that a shadow factory was set up lower down Tolpits Lane in 1940 and this became known as the Moor Park Works. This plant was extended in 1941 and was later designated as the main trailer works wherein they produced a wide range of trailers for both military use and for allocation to those road hauliers who could prove to the ministry that they had an approved need for one. It is an oft-quoted fact that for every tractor unit fitted with a Scammell coupling at least two trailers would also be supplied.

By the 1950s it seemed that almost every self-respecting haulage company owned at least one Scammell combination. The benefits of automatic coupling were also perceived to be a major advantage by many thousands of 'C' licence operators.

Above: *The frameless tanker concept displayed to good effect on this Mackeson Stout tanker. To save weight and also lower the centre of gravity, the coupling gear and rear axle are mounted directly on the tank shell. This is a mid-1950s model since the under carriage wheels have 5 holes rather than the four holes on the earlier versions.* Mechanical Horse Club

Often these companies, who could only carry their own goods, made use of the simple fact that whilst one trailer was being loaded a second trailer could be unloading and have a third in transit, yet all be served by a single tractor unit. The automatic coupling was just as popular within the 'for reward' haulage sector where vehicles operated under 'A' or 'B' licences. In loose terms, the 'A' licence enabled a haulier to carry goods anywhere, but the licences were difficult to obtain.

The 'B' licence was far more restrictive in that it often specified the type of goods to be carried or the area in which the vehicle could work. It would take a further volume of this book to describe the variety of operators, vehicle and trailer combinations involved, but the reader can be assured that the companies involved covered virtually every spectrum of British industry from international road haulage to internal works transport. As the obvious advantages of the automatic coupling came to the notice of the industry an even greater number of truck manufacturers began to offer a chassis that was suitable for conversion to an articulated tractor with a Scammell coupling. Of course the Bedford name was at the forefront, closely followed by Commer. Strangely enough the other major mass producer Ford, were very slow in offering suitable tractor units. The Fordson 7V was occasionally modified to pull trailers and the later Thames models could be seen with Carrimore or BTC trailers using a fifth wheel.

It was not until Ford introduced their groundbreaking Trader in 1959 that the short wheelbase tractor unit became a regular production option, along with a chassis suitably modified to suit the automatic coupling. The companies that came to make up BMC, notably Austin and Morris did not offer a factory-built chassis suitable for conversion until the normal control Loadstar model was in production. The forward control 7-ton models that BMC later introduced also became a very popular base for conversion to a tractor unit, and these were again used in many types of industry. Most of the tractor units at the time boasted a wheelbase between 8ft 0in and 8ft 6in and the short wheelbase combined with stiff springing guaranteed a lively ride for the driver when the tractor unit was solo or pulling an unladen trailer. The rear of the chassis was always substantially modified to fit the relatively low mounting of the automatic coupling.

Top Left: *The British Motor Corporation were major users of automatic coupling trailers. This photograph of an Austin Loadstar and van trailer clearly displays the absence of landing legs on the trailer when coupled up to the tractor*

Centre Left: *It is very hard to define the most popular use for the system within road transport, BRS for example inherited a large number of automatic coupling tractors and continued to purchase similar vehicles. This is a Dodge/Scammell unit prior to delivery.*

Bottom Left: *One of the many Leyland Comet tractors fitted with Scammell coupling gear is shown on demonstration duties at Watford goods depot carrying some 'borrowed' packing cases. These Comets shared the same basic Briggs built cab as the Dodge shown above.*

Top Right: *One of the many thousands of automatic coupling van trailers used by BRS Parcels, who were later to become Roadline parcels. These trailers could be used for daytime collection and delivery work and overnight trunking between depots. The coupling gear was of the later non-collapsible type. The van body was built by the nationalised concern of Star bodies in Hollinwood near Oldham.*

The range of trailers and bodies in use was absolutely remarkable: from box vans to flats, from furniture vans to step frames and from refrigerated vans to pole carriers. In fact if it was not in the catalogue then Scammells would simply design one for you, but we should point out that the 'standard' range of Scammell trailers comprised about 600 different types!

Within the railway fleet alone one could find the following trailer types: - flat platform, dropside, tipper, extendable platform, pole trailer, half-tilt van, full-tilt van, vanesta (these were wire mesh sided bodies), glass carrier, drop frame and step frame trailers of various types, and cable drum carriers, as well as a variety of vans with differing sizes and door positions. Primarily designed for short-haul work, the Scammell units came to be used as trunk vehicles in their own right giving a very cost effective 8-ton unit for not much more

than the cost of a 4-tonner. Despite the trailers' basic simplicity there were a couple of problems that only manifested themselves after considerable use. The brass to brass electrical contacts between tractor and trailer would tend to wear and if an unladen trailer was driven along a bumpy road then the rear lights would tend to go on and off as the contacts moved relative to each other. The other fault came about if the tractor and trailer were only infrequently disconnected and the trailer undercarriage had not been regularly lubricated. As the tractor unit drove away from the trailer, the undercarriage would fail to 'unlock' and the trailer would fall on its knees! To be able to spot a genuine Scammell trailer the simple clue was to note the front of the trailer, because the lower front corners of the chassis frame were chamfered to give clearance when coupling under extreme conditions.

Chapter 7. The Egyptian Beetle

With the ending of the war demand for all types of lorry increased and Scammell's were no exception, but much of their early post war production was destined for export and UK domestic orders came far down the list of urgent demands. However, the management at Watford were well aware that the Mechanical Horse in its original form was no match for the post-war market demands and set about redesigning the 'horse without losing its major benefits. The major shortcomings of the old design included, no self-starter, and a very basic but relatively expensive coachbuilt wooden cab with little pretensions to comfort, especially for the passenger. Added to these factors was the aforementioned embarrassing tendency for the 'horse to fall on to its side on sharp right hand turns due to a combination of a high centre of gravity and the offset engine. Any replacement for the mechanical horse had to remain true to the original concept of a highly manoeuvrable 3-wheel tractor unit and as such the main design details were almost pre-ordained. This was especially important in view of the huge number of automatic coupling trailers already in existence and the fact that the new vehicle obviously had to remain compatible with those trailers.

Top Left: *A typical view of a BR Scammell Scarab, pictured on the weighbridge at Berkhamstead, with a load of Bass beer that driver Shaw will be taking to the King's Arms Hotel.* A. Delderfield

What transpired in 1948 was an altogether different breed of creature from the original 'horse. Whilst retaining the original 3-wheel layout and the essentials of the coupling gear almost everything else changed for the better. The major change from the original 'horse, but similar to the little prototype 30cwt horse, was the mounting of the engine low down in the chassis behind the cab. This gave the immediate advantage of both lowering the centre of gravity and increasing the weight on the rear axle to improve traction capability. In turn this enabled the engine, gearbox and rear axle to be combined in one easily removed unit. The engine was secured to the chassis front by a large bolt with rubber bushes and through the spring hangers at the rear. Access to the engine's cylinder head and ancillaries were via a 'bonnet', which was attached to the cab rear panel and sat on the top of the chassis. The major components of the coupling gear were retained, but integrated far more with the chassis, and again there were two sizes of coupling gear for 3-ton and 6-ton loads.

Originally fitted with a manually operated braking system, an important change was the incorporation of vacuum assistance on the trailer brakes in 1951! However, the rear wheel brakes on the tractor units remained rod-operated. The rear suspension of the tractor unit retained leaf springs, though these were now slipper ended. The single front wheel that gave the vehicle its remarkable turning circle was given an oil-filled damper to replace the simple coil springs of its predecessor.

Because of the unique chassis design of mid-mounted engine and single front wheel the radiator could not be fitted in the front of the vehicle. Instead it was in fact placed in front of the engine and mounted in the rear wall of the cab, which (unfortunately for the driver) could get rather warm at times. The central placing of the radiator meant that the gear lever could not retain its normal central position, so it was placed within a gate on the right hand side of the driver's seat. In front of the driver were the pedals and three levers, one each for the tractor and trailer handbrakes and a third for uncoupling the trailer. The steering wheel was of necessity mounted almost vertically. Once the chassis design was completed all that was required was a cab to fit.

At the time of the planning of this new tractor the Scammell company was still working closely with Bedford on the fitting of 6-ton coupling gear to the Bedford OSS tractor chassis. As a result it was decided to use parts of the standard Bedford cab pressings as a basis for the cab of the new 3-wheeler. In fact this cab structure was also used on quite a variety of larger Scammells during the 1950s with alterations to the length of the cab doors and to the rear cab panels. The Willenhall Motor & Radiator Company, a major supplier of components to the motor industry over a long period, manufactured the cab components. With a need to supply the mid-mounted radiator with a flow of cooling air, a grille and associated ducting were fitted on the offside rear panel of the cab behind the drivers door, allowing a rounded nose of Scammell design to finish off the cab. In view of the potential for higher speeds with this new tractor it came fitted with a speedometer as well as an ammeter and could also boast warning lights for low oil pressure and later for low vacuum. The final problem was what to call the new tractor. The decision to combine the names of the best breeds of commercial vehicle and horse resulted in the glorious combination of SCAmmell and ARAB to become the SCARAB. Yet it has been said that the way these vehicles scurried about in busy yards did remind one of the Egyptian Scarab beetle.

Initially only one engine size was offered on the Scarab, 2090cc four-cylinder petrol engine, yet by fitting different carburettors, this could give either 34hp or 45hp. The earlier Scarabs came fitted with a Scintilla Magneto, but a coil and distributor soon became a production standard. Drive was again to a double reduction rear axle through a four-speed constant mesh gearbox produced by David Brown's of Huddersfield. Various axle ratios were available but the standard ratios were 9.65 to 1 and 11.23 to 1 for the 3-ton and 6-ton models respectively. These ratios reflected the higher power available as well as the need for higher road speeds and compared favourably with the standard ratios of 10.28 to 1 and a fearsome optional 19.44 to 1 that were used in the smaller and larger Mechanical Horses respectively.

DESIGNED AND BUILT BY
THE STEEL BARREL Co. Ltd.,
UXBRIDGE, MIDDX., ENGLAND

Above: *This wonderful contraption would certainly turn the head of any modern motorist, with what appears to be a mobile petrol station. This 3-ton Scarab petrol dispenser was of a type used for supplying fuel at docks and airports. The tanker was designed and built by the Steel Barrel Co. in Uxbridge, Middlesex and usually carried a Hardol petrol pump located directly above the rear axle. Two of these were used at Heathrow Airport as fuel bowsers for the supply of other airport service vehicles. Others were known to have been used at Southampton Docks and Southend Airport!* Scammell Lorries

Below: *Like its predecessor the Scarab could be ordered as a rigid load carrier. In this instance the Borough of Barry chose the ultimate in manoeuvrability for use as a refuse collection vehicle and fitted it with a 2-bay Chelsea (or chip-pan lid) style body.*

Above: *This picture was issued by Scammell on 13th November 1948, with the vehicle registration number blacked out. It showed what looked to be a truly continental scene, with twin headlights and a Carlsberg grain transporter, but as will be seen it was in fact a UK registered lorry. It is probably a very early 6-ton (left hand drive) Scarab, and may well be a prototype. Note the fact that the front bumper is bolted through the bodywork, whilst the gutter above the door extends beyond and behind the door to the radiator grill. The headlight fairings also differ from later models.* Mechanical Horse Club

Below: *Here we see another 6-ton Scarab, this time fitted with a diesel engine for the arduous task of towing around this heavy mobile library trailer used by the Borough of East Ham. It is hoped to produce a future* **Nostalgia Road** *book on travelling libraries, and if any reader has information on this subject we would welcome their assistance.* Mechanical Horse Club

The Scarab became even more successful than its illustrious predecessor had been, and from its debut in 1948 it sold over 13,000 models before it finally ceased production in 1967. At least one prototype lightweight Scarab was built in 1947. No real details are known of its engine or chassis, though it definitely used smaller components all round than the standard Scarab parts. It certainly boasted a folding door to the passenger side and was probably built to carry a 30-cwt load. Its only real claim to fame is in being photographed outside Watford Metropolitan station with a 1920s London Transport 'T' stock electric multiple unit train in the background.

There were very few mechanical changes to the Scarab during its long life. A diesel option became widely available from the mid-1950s with Perkins supplying their 4.99 engine for the 3-tonner from May 1959. For the 6-ton Scarab the first diesel option offered was the Perkins P4 engine from September 1956 and the modernised Perkins 4.203 supplanted this engine in April 1963. The lateness in offering the diesel option had its roots in the low mileage covered by these units in service. Within the nationalised BR sundries operation the fuel savings possible on an average daily mileage of 25-40 miles were not equal to the higher initial purchase cost nor to the perceived complications of a diesel engine. Attitudes eventually changed and diesels became the normal production specification. Visually with the Scarabs there was even less variety than there was with the original mechanical horses. Tyre and wheel sizes 8.25-10 all round were standard on the 3-ton model while the 6-ton variant would normally have 10.50-13 tyres at the rear. An option was twin 700-20 tyres at the rear but these were mainly fitted on the few rigid vehicles that were built.

The cabs hardly changed except that models built for the Government and for export to Europe boasted twin headlamps rather than the single headlamp specified for British use and the nameplate also altered depending upon final destination. The only other obvious external change was the addition of flashing indicators normally fitted on stalks mounted on the roof sides in the 1960s. The idea of this high mounting was to give a warning of the driver's intentions to following traffic over the top of trailers, which may not have had any indicators fitted. In fact the fitting of flashing trafficators to the railway lorry fleet was a major logistical exercise in itself. The railway management had to cope with the possibility of either the unit or trailer having or not having indicators during the changeover period. The major problem would occur when a trailer fitted with indicator lenses was pulled by a tractor unit as yet unfitted. The simple answer was for the trailer to have lens covers that were fitted in the form of a drop-down flap! This, it was hoped, would protect following motorists from disaster.

Just like the Mechanical Horse before it, the Scarab sold to an enormous variety of buyers. BR bought about 7,500 vehicles but the tractor could be found in virtually every town and village serving with national operators like British Road Services and the GPO. Smaller fleets were operated, by industrial manufacturers, retailers, brewers, municipalities and even the BBC. In the early 1950s with an export or die philosophy lead by the Government Scammell Lorries certainly played their part.

The Scarab was also quite capable of selling itself abroad especially to Commonwealth countries where administration of the railways or municipalities remained in British hands. Notable users were the East African Railway companies and certain Indian and Ceylonese local authorities amongst very many others.

The British Government continued to purchase 3-wheel tractors in both forms of the Scarab, mainly for use in ordnance and army depots, but around 200 were also to be found on RAF bases and in the maintenance units. For example RAF 22MU at Carlisle had no less than 20 Scarabs at one time, and nearby RAF 15MU at Silloth had a dozen more. The Royal Navy used them in their stores, and dockyards, and even had some serving at sea in various aircraft carriers.

Ironically at the same time that the Ministry of Defence was ordering new Scarabs, the Army and RAF were auctioning off large numbers of their older, (and often little used) Mechanical Horses. These ex-MoD horses were snapped up by industry, and they could often be found working alongside new Scarabs in many factories. One prime example of this was the Grimsby Ice Co., who bought about a dozen ex-RAF tractor units and converted most of them to battery-electric operation to handle its fleet of trailers supplying ice to the Grimsby deep sea trawler fleet and the local fish merchants. One new Scarab was purchased, but it was outlasted by most of the Mechanical Horses since the its cab rusted away in the corrosive salty atmosphere of Grimsby Docks.

Like the Mechanical Horse, the Scarab also came to be offered in rigid form, although there were only a few built. Some became rigid dustcarts both in Britain and abroad, but perhaps the most unlikely pair became breakdown trucks at the new Dartford Tunnel under the River Thames in the early-1960s. With their unequalled turning circle they were ideal for use in the 21ft width carriageways of the tunnels and proved themselves capable of recovering vehicles of up to 7-tons gross. Luckily both of these rare beasts have been rescued for preservation. The success of these Scarabs did not go unnoticed since a similar pair was supplied to Hong Kong in 1965 for use in the Lion Rock Tunnel.

Of all the trailers in municipal use perhaps the most bizarre was the articulated road sweeper. This consisted of a Scarab tractor unit connected to a self-contained sweeper and collector trailer. In fact the trailer was so self contained that it had its own dedicated operator, who sat out in the open on top of the bodywork controlling the actual sweeping operation. One hopes that the driver and operator were on good terms!

Some of the London borough councils and corporations also used articulated tanker street washers with a separate engine and operator, again with the operator exposed to the elements. In Liverpool a large fleet of Scarabs were used in conjunction with 'step frame barrier' refuse collection bodies. These were special in that the floor level was lower than usual and when the bodies tipped for discharge, the trailer wheel boxes retracted to allow the refuse to flow out unhindered. In many areas this style of refuse collection vehicle was quite popular. In the days before purpose-built gritting lorries, many refuse trailers were loaded with sand on frosty nights and the gritting crew stood on the rear step and shovelled the grit onto the icy roads.

Above: *As will be seen from the cab-side lettering this pair of Scarabs was destined for the warmer climes of Nigeria in the early-1950s. One has to assume that the brewery transport manager in Lagos was aware just how capable the Scarabs could be whilst working on urban deliveries, but one wonders what urban duties they would have worked, and how long they actually remained at working in a country where commercial trucks had great longevity.* Scammell Lorries

Below: *One of the pair of Dartford Tunnel rescue trucks referred to in the text. They were based on modified Scarab chassis complete with twin 7.00-20 rear wheels and carried front mounted counter balance weights. They were comprehensively equipped for most emergencies.* Geoff Arnold

Learning to drive the 3-wheeled articulated trucks was not easy, and reversing was a specifically difficult task until the 'knack' was learnt. The railway companies had their own training schools, but as staff shortages arose in the 1950s many other railwaymen were pressed into service after the minimum amount of training. Perhaps the reminiscences of Mr. R Harris will suffice to explain the problems. He joined British Railways at Brighton in 1964 as a porter, but rapidly progressed to driving rigid vehicles. He was soon given the opportunity to try his hand at driving both Scarabs and Bantams. His first comment about the Scarab was that if you did not notice the position of the front wheel when approaching the vehicle, then when you let the clutch in you had the disconcerting sensation of going sideways if the steering had been left on full lock. For several weeks Mr. Harris practiced reversing the trailer, which of course had a mind of its own. He continues 'I remember one day reversing the trailer end on to a rail wagon, the rear of the trailer swung round straight up to the doors, dead square, tractor in line, perfect. The fact was that it wasn't against the wagon I had intended, was beside the point!

Top Left: *In this trio of pictures we can illustrate the diversity of trailers employed within the British Railways operation. This brand new BR (Midland Region) 6 ton Scarab was photographed for publicity purposes at the Scammell works coupled to a BR (Western Region) 20ft dropside trailer. In real life, it would be very unusual to find a tractor unit from one region, hauling a trailer from another, but it did happen in some cities from time to time, or when transfers took place before a vehicle was given a new fleet number, but this was the exception rather than the rule.*

Centre Left: *In London the movement of parcels between the various terminal stations was undertaken by a fleet of Scarabs used in conjunction with a large number of dedicated 3-ton van trailers all identified with the distinctive black and white chequer markings. This view shows a Western Region Scarab 34298W with a Western Region transfer trailer T5844W; the 'T' standing for transfer trailer, the 'W' indicating Western Region.*

Bottom Left*: The railways with their need to provide transport facilities for a wide range of goods employed a number of float trailers for the movement of sheet or plate glass. In this instance a drop frame float trailer is coupled to a brand new 3-ton Scarab. This trailer was just one of the 600 standard designs available from Scammell at the time and we should not forget that the originators of the principle, the railways, were buying these trailers by the thousand.*

Top Right: *The delightful picture of the Scammell Scarab shown opposite is highly representative of the type of work undertaken by this remarkable vehicle. Operated by Chesters Brewery of Ardwick, Manchester its daily work was delivering bottled products to typical working class public houses in the city. In fact, the pub shown here could almost be the prototype 'Rover's Return' in Coronation Street!*

Chapter 8. Industrial Use

There are many instances of the Scammell coupling being used in industry, but a very well written article was printed in the early-1950s (outlining the intricacies of manufacturing electric cables) extolling the virtue of the Scammell system. Set in a Lancashire factory, part of the article is reproduced here, courtesy of the British Insulated Calendars Cables company. 'It is generally accepted that in the case of a shuttle service one mechanical horse can effectively operate with two or three trailers. This reduces standing time for the driver and provides a steady flow of work with minimum waiting periods. These benefits are accepted in industry but it is rare to find the entire short haul and internal transport service of a large manufacturing company based on the full use of tractor units in conjunction with a wide variety of semi-trailers to suit all departments of the factory's activities. A striking example of this type of operation is to be seen at the Leigh, Lancashire, works of the B.I.C.C. Company, where from 1937 the transport manager has developed the system to a high standard.

The works at Leigh are scattered over an area of 25 acres and have two miles of internal roadway. There is no single production line as such due to the multiplicity of cable types produced; thus a considerable volume of internal transport between departments and stores is necessary. These conditions led to the purchase of the first Mechanical Horse in 1937 and the system has been built up on the basis of 'plenty of semi trailers in as many varieties as possible'. The fleet now consists of eight tractor units and 31 trailers although not all are taxed for external use. The trailers consisted of a variety of flats and low loaders along with some tippers for the haulage of coal from the local wharves and some small box vans. The articulation concept offers much greater operational flexibility compared to a rigid vehicle based operation.

The trailers can be left to be loaded at a time to suit the department concerned, and can in fact be used as mobile store rooms and even hold outgoing goods until the railway is ready to receive them. The small box vans have a 2-ton capacity and their main function is for use as wheeled containers for small production components.

So successful has the detachable trailer system been in the internal and short haul sphere, that it is now used for journeys to branch offices and customers within a 30 mile radius. Outward loads however are, in the main, to the local railway goods yards, to the Liverpool docks and to the firm's other factories in Prescot and Helsby. Long distance deliveries not suited to the railways are carried out by the firm's own rigid vehicles and by hired transport, but will soon change to be based on the Scammell system. This will bring to the delivery system similar savings to those made in the factory. For example the current 12-ton Leyland lorry and trailer makes a regular exchange of products with the London factory. This takes four days; two days travelling and one day each for loading and unloading at each factory. With the new system an exchange of trailers at each end of the journey will enable a 25% saving to be made by reducing the job to just three days'.

There are a few comments worth noting from this article. Firstly, the comment about coals being collected from the wharves. The town of Leigh was based in the centre of the Lancashire coalfield and many of the local mines had direct access to the Bridgewater Canal that also ran alongside the BICC works. This canal had the distinction of being the first major artificial waterway in industrial England. The second comment concerns the use of the railway for the delivery of goods, note just how commonplace it was back in the 1950s. Finally note how long it used to take to drive from Lancashire to London!

It was not only the management at BICC who realised just how effective the automatic coupling system was in the days before the universal introduction of the fork lift truck. Many companies with production facilities spread over a wide area or diverse sites found the system ideal. Two other examples were Courtaulds in Coventry and Rylands Wire in Warrington. In London Bryant & May found Scarabs ideal for the shuttle movement of trailers carrying imported poplar logs for match making. In Colchester the Davey Paxman Company fitted their Scarab with a two-way radio in the early-1950s to make best use of the flexibility of the tractor unit and numerous trailers, whilst the Manchester Ship Canal Company found them irreplaceable. The versatile trailers had their uses in other dockland areas.

Top Left: *In the days before tail lifts "lorry loaders" were often used. In this case a miniature crane is being used to load a heavy cable drum onto a Leyland Comet and trailer at the Leigh works of B.I.C.C.*

Centre Left: *The Manchester Ship Canal Company used a fleet of Scarabs for the collection and delivery of goods in the Manchester and Warrington areas. They used a ratio of three trailers to one Scarab to allow trailers to stand whilst being loaded. They had another great benefit, to quote the company transport manager in 1958 'they get in places where other types of vehicle can't'. Now where have I heard that before?*

Bottom Left: *This 6-ton Scarab and tipping trailer were used for the delivery of coke from Taunton Gas works. Note the scorch marks on the coke hopper where the contents had caught fire.*

Chapter 9. Competitors

It should not be assumed that Karrier and Scammell had the complete monopoly on the production of small-articulated units, for competition will always spring up where a successful concept is found. The mechanical horse was no exception, and possibly the first (and certainly the least likely) contender came from the Ford stable in the form of the 3-wheeled Fordson Tug. This vehicle was more of a works tug than a haulage unit and featured a car like design with a long bonnet, car doors and a very basic agricultural style rear hitch.

It was derived from the very successful Model 'Y' passenger car and was intended for use with the type of trailer normally associated with Fordson industrial tractors. At the time when Ford were planning this vehicle, the plant at Dagenham did not have the appropriate design facilities so development of the Tug was entrusted to County Commercial Cars Ltd. This company was to become quite famous for their 4-wheel drive conversions to Fordson tractors and earlier to Fordson Commercial Vehicles with their Surrey and Sussex 6-wheeler conversions. Despite Ford's formidable marketing it soon became clear that the designers had conceived a 'white elephant' rather than a Mechanical Horse.

Above: *The 3-wheelers tractors that were built under licence in France were very modern in comparison to their British brothers. This 1955 view shows a FAR CM70F fitted with a Hispano 4 cyl 4190cc Diesel engine, a Ford F52 4 speed gearbox and an Eaton 2 speed rear axle in addition to the tilt cab, which gave easy access to the engine.* Scammell Lorries

The Tug was available from 1935 to the autumn of 1937, at which time the model Y car was superseded and production of the Tug came to an end after a miserly 125 units had been built. The mechanical specification of the Tug was similar to the car, with a 933cc side valve petrol engine and a torque tube/radius arm rear axle. The main difference was of course the single coil sprung front wheel and there was also a four-speed gearbox. The prototype Ford Tug appeared in the summer of 1935 and arrangements were put in hand for production at Dagenham. The public launch of the vehicle was in September 1935 with the usual hullabaloo.

Perhaps the most telling point about this vehicle was that the trailer coupling gear was similar to that fitted to the Fordson 'N' agricultural tractor and this immediately ruled it out as a competitor to the established mechanical horses.

Above: *The City of Westminster operated this articulated gully emptier. Built by Electricar it was based on the Mechanical Horse and featured battery electric power for both traction purposes and for the exhauster that created a vacuum in the Dennis-built semi-trailer tank.* Mechanical Horse Club

Below: *Pictured at Dewsbury in the heart of the heavy woollen district in the West Riding of Yorkshire, this early MkI Jen Tug is carrying what looks like a capacity load. The large hessian sack undoubtedly contains a load of shoddy, this was woollen materials being returned for re-processing. The wicker baskets were the property of the United Cloth Combing Company, again another firm that re-processed woollen waste, and produced a heavy wool cloth that was used for army great coats. The goods yard seen here is that located on the old Great Northern line from Wakefield to Batley and Bradford.* Mechanical Horse Club

A number of Scammell Mechanical Horses came to be converted from new by Partridge Wilson of Leicester into battery driven tractor units, mainly, (but not exclusively) for municipal use. These battery electric vehicles were marketed as Wilson Scammells and the smaller model was advertised as being suitable for the movement of 4-ton loads. In addition Birmingham-based Electricar Ltd. produced a number of battery electric 'horses for Westminster City Council. At first glance these looked like the normal Scammell Mechanical Horse, but in fact the cab design varied quite considerably. These worked in conjunction with a variety of trailers including refuse collectors, gully emptiers, water sprinklers and refuse compression trailers which featured a mechanically driven compaction device.

There were 26 Electricar TV model 'horses working in conjunction with about 14 petrol MH's, and these battery vehicles had a working life that was 10 years longer than their petrol-driven brothers. Replacements for the electric vehicles came in the early 1960s and featured Dennis Pax IV battery electric tractors using motors from the old Electricars! The requirement for electric tractors was driven by a need for quiet operation at night since the corporation worked round the clock and the up-market residents of Westminster had no wish to be awoken from their slumbers by a mere dustcart!

Just before the war a company based in Wiltshire trading under the name of Rawlence produced a small 4-wheel petrol driven articulated tractor unit fitted with just one central ramp for the rather unusual automatic coupling gear. Although advertised widely only one vehicle seems to have been built and it was operated by a railway cartage agent named Thomas Bantock of Wolverhampton who at the time operated a number of standard Scammell Mechanical Horses. Design of this vehicle had been in the hands of ex-Latil Industrial Vehicles staff and the coupling is thought to have originated with the Staussler Company.

Shortly after the war the Jensen Company (of car fame) took on a Mr. Riekie who had been employed by Latil as an engineer and demonstrator. The Jensen Company was involved with the transformation of the Rawlence tractor into the Jensen Jen Tug ART MkI. This was very similar in layout to the Rawlence, built to carry 30-40 cwt loads originally utilising a Ford 10hp side-valve petrol engine and three-speed column change gearbox, both mounted in a subframe to allow simple removal. It was able to boast 4-wheel hydraulic brakes and a low step, easy entry cab. Actually the cab doors were forward opening (i.e. rear hinged) and came to be commonly referred to as suicide doors! In 1952 the ART MkII was introduced and it featured an Austin A40 1200cc 4-cylinder ohv engine governed to 35bhp.

The engine was mounted as before (complete with clutch and gearbox in a subframe), but this time the engine was moved rearwards to increase traction. The gearbox was the standard Austin four-speed and was controlled by a gear lever mounted on the steering column. At the same time as the fitting of the new engine the carrying capacity was increased from 2½- to 3-tons. A diesel engine in the form of the BMC 2.2 litre was made available for the ART MkIII in 1954, but apparently this did not sell well. Instead a 1489cc petrol engine came to be fitted in to the MkII model in 1955.

The coupling gear was unique to the Jen Tug and looked like a half Scammell coupling utilising just the single central ramp. With the trailer jockey wheels being placed outside the unit's rear wheels the rear track of the Tug was so narrow that a differential was not considered essential on the early models. In fact the rear axle track was a mere 2ft 5in. The turning circle of the Jen Tug and trailer was a creditable 22 feet and could be reduced by shunting to 18 feet.

The production span of the Jen Tug continued through to 1957 by which time it was realised that there was not a large enough market for such a specialised small vehicle in a market already dominated by the Scammell Scarab and the Karrier Bantam. Its demise was also hastened by the use of many car-derived components as these did not last long in the hands of lorry drivers. However, in the hands of sympathetic drivers, these little vehicles lasted into the 1960s on certain areas of the Eastern Region of British Railways. The firm of Hindle Smart in Manchester converted some new chassis to battery-electric traction and sold them as Jen Helecs. Several battery electric vehicle manufacturers also offered tractor versions of their normal 2-ton vans. These came to be used in small numbers by British Railways, but mostly in places like Hull and York where there were few gradients to cause them problems. Involved with the manufacture of the electric horses were companies such as Brush, Morrison and Crompton Parkinson.

The Karrier Bantam itself was upgraded to MkIII status in 1950 when the old wooden framed cab was replaced by the rather futuristic steel cab from the Commer range and the petrol engine was uprated in the form of a 2266cc Rootes group design. The MkIII Bantam was able to boast a four speed syncromesh gearbox from 1953 and in the following year the Perkins P4 diesel engine was available as an option. Although the Bantam was considered a more stable vehicle than the 3-wheelers, it was not quite the panacea that the Rootes Group thought it was going to be. The haulage origins of the vehicle meant that the engine was placed too far forward in the chassis to be ideal for a short wheelbase tractor unit. This contributed to poor weight distribution, which meant that the vehicle could be rather a handful in inclement conditions. Much later, when the Bantam range began showing its age (and was eventually discontinued), British Railways obtained a Commer Walk-thru chassis/cab with a Scammell automatic coupling for evaluation, but nothing came of it.

If any one particular truck can be considered to be the direct descendant of the Bantam it must be Ford's baby artic, the tiny D series model designated DA300. These came to be bought in large numbers by National Carriers who by that time had become part of the National Freight Corporation. In this case the coupling gear was designed and built by Taskers, yet it remained totally compatible with the Scammell 3-ton gear. The National Carriers purchasing department must have been well satisfied with the Ford D series range since a lot more of the larger models began to enter service fitted with 6-ton coupling gear. Since the 'D' series featured both a tilt cab and 'cross-cab' access for the driver, the engine was placed under the cab at the rear, in Scarab fashion, and this gave better weight distribution and therefore greater stability.

Above: *Looking slightly more modern with its maroon and cream livery is this MKII Jen Tug seen in London in the mid fifties. The difference in track widths between front and rear axles is discernible in this picture. The van trailer was of very similar construction to those used behind the Scarabs, though the coupling was totally different.* Mechanical Horse Club

Below: *When the National Freight Corporation was established in 1968 it took over the British Railways Sundries operation and renamed it National Carriers. A smart new, modern-looking logo was designed to reflect a 'speed image' and added to the yellow liveried vehicles. Yet this did little to inspire customer confidence, as many still retained BR liveries until their turn came for a repaint. This former Scottish Region 3-ton Karrier Bantam is shown in the new NCL livery hauling a 5-ton twin wheeled parcels van, probably in Dundee.* Phil Moth

CHAPTER 10. PROGRESS AND 4-WHEELERS

In 1955 the Scammell Company were taken over by Leyland Motors which later proved to be a significant event with the eventual closure of the works. At first no obvious signs of change overwhelmed the Watford factory. Gradually more Leyland components came to be used in Scammell vehicles, but more importantly more Leyland Group lorry chassis came to Watford to be converted to automatic coupling. Up till the early-1950s the most common conversions had been on the lightweight chassis such as Bedford or Commer, now the market was turning to the higher quality vehicles such as Leyland and Albion for conversion to tractors. Most makers only offered factory built cabs by this period, but Albion held to the principle that the buyer could choose his own cab builder. As a result many Albion chassis were delivered to Scammell's by ferry drivers wearing ex-army greatcoats, goggles and a flying helmet to protect them on the trip from Glasgow. Even so, having traversed Beattock and Shap on the journey south, they would often arrive in Watford frozen half to death.

Above: *A Mk.V Karrier Bantam with J type coupling bought by British Railways in 1964, and repainted into the National Carriers livery in 1970. The van trailer has 7.00-20 tyres, giving a higher floor level to line up with loading bays.* Mechanical Horse Club

This period also confirmed that the move to articulation in fleets was not just for the increase in carrying capacity over rigid vehicles, but the greater realisation that pre-loaded trailers were a great boon. This pre-loading ensured that the expensive tractor unit was fully utilised, and many operators made use of the expensive tractor units day and night. A prime example of better utilisation was on the short sea ferry crossing to Northern Ireland from Preston where virtually every load was handled by automatic coupling trailers with the tractor units delivering and collecting the trailers from the docks.

To give customers quicker delivery times of new tractor chassis, whilst it was still on their production line. Complete kits of component would be despatched from Watford to the appropriate factory. Both the Guy and the Thornycroft factories regularly used this option.

This certainly was the case with Thornycroft, Dennis and Albion, though how prevalent this practice was is open to question. In addition various other trailer manufacturers would buy the Scammell coupling gear and trailer axles to put under their own chassis.

Another intriguing sight during this period concerned the delivery of trailers (mainly the smaller 3-ton variety) to British Railways. At this time BR had extensive body building facilities and would tend to order just the basic trailer chassis fitted with cross-members and a perimeter frame to allow any type of body to be fitted. Most of these trailers were despatched via the nearest suitable station which, in this case, was Watford Metropolitan. Here the joint LNER/Metropolitan Company had established a goods yard and the trailers would be bought in pairs (laid platform to platform) and reversed up the cattle ramp and onto BR Conflat wagons for despatch by the train load! If any reader has a photo of this operation could they please contact the author via the publishers? Throughout the life of the automatic coupling on the railways, there were always two separate types of 3-ton platform trailer. The earliest tended to have a slightly higher platform because they used single 7.00-20 tyres. Later models were fitted with the same 8.25-10 tyres on single wheels as the motive unit and would often be built to a slightly lower overall height than the earlier versions.

Right through the 1950s and into the 1960s the automatic coupling remained in great favour. Brockhouse, BTC, Hands and Taskers amongst others brought out alternative versions and were more or less compatible and interchangeable. Rather like the Karrier coupling design of the 1930s the couplings used by Hands and Taskers both utilised 'C' shaped clamps to hold the flanged wheels in place. All of the coupling gear would look similar, but they had a number of differences, mainly involved with the design and look of the coupling ramps themselves. The overall payload was gradually increased by all the makers to 12-tons and undercarriages were modified so as not to collapse/retract on uncoupling. The benefits remained with the ease and speed of changing over trailers and the wide variety of trailers available.

The overall design of the coupling gear hardly changed over a 50-year period. Obviously materials improved, and better manufacturing methods were found, but even today a 1933 trailer will couple to a 1970s tractor. The trailer layout hardly changed either. Most trailers remained fitted with just a single axle, the Scammell version of which was slightly cambered and was designed to ensure that the wheels remained parallel to the road when the trailer was fully laden. Brakes on the trailer remained cable operated from the turntable to the axle until the advent of the plating regulations, which then required additional secondary braking facilities with air or vacuum operating cylinders being mounted on the trailer axle in addition to those on the tractor unit. This of course meant that the driver had to leave his cab to couple up the air or vacuum lines, but the actual coupling operation still remained quick and simple. During the late-1960s Scammell introduced the MkIII coupling gear which featured a retractable, but non-collapsible undercarriage. It was fitted with much smaller landing wheels, and was very similar to the type built by Hands and Taskers, that had been introduced some years earlier.

Above: *This is the 8/10-ton automatic coupling as fitted to a Commer tractor chassis. The main items to note are the lack of a rear cross-member and the replacement strengthening stays. Also clearly shown are the twin hooks to hold the trailer in place, along with the trailer brake operating slipper between them. Beneath the brake slipper is the tongue that forced the trailer undercarriage to retract on coupling.* Scammell Lorries

Below: *This photograph shows a Bedford TK with the Hands version of the coupling that does not use twin hooks to retain the trailer, but relied on clamping the small flanged wheels that were fitted on the trailer turntable.* Vauxhall Motors

Above: *This new unit was given the completely uninspiring title of 'The Scarab Four', and from the outside it looked ungainly. The cab was narrow in comparison with the trailers it was meant to pull, and the front track was even narrower compared with the unit's rear axle track. Fitted with a Karrier-type BK coupling, this was one of 60 supplied to South African Railways.*

Below: *The Scarab 4 always looked 'under-tyred'! It is a good thing that few people saw how the Standard front and Scammell rear were actually put together underneath the cab, for it was certainly not one of the Watford company's best efforts at engineering prowess. One amazing feature that was carried over from the Standard Atlas/Leyland 20 was the inclusion of a cab heater as standard, possibly the first small Scammell ever to have such a luxury. This model is fitted with a Scammell coupling.* Both Mechanical Horse Club.

By the early 1960s it was recognised that sales of the 3-wheel tractor units were gradually declining. This was mainly due to the fact that the major customer for these units, British Railways, was altering the system by which rail freight sundries and smalls were being handled. It was also due in part to the fact that additional sales of the Scarab were being jeopardised by the perceived inherent lack of stability of its 3-wheels. The sales people thought that they had better look at a model to challenge the four-wheel Karrier Bantam tractor unit, which was still the only real competitor to the Scarab.

By this time Scammell had been totally swallowed up into the Leyland empire and amongst the models sold by the group was the Standard Atlas van (later known as the Leyland 20). Now this van was hardly what one would call a best seller, but it did have the advantage of being fitted with a diesel engine that had a long pedigree and was by now known as the Leyland OE138 2.26 litre. The front end of the van was considered by Leyland management as being the suitable base for a 4-wheel tractor.

So Scammell were lumbered with trying to make a silk purse out of a sow's ear by trying to build a competitive 4-wheeled tractor unit for 3-ton loads using the best parts of the Scarab and Atlas. In fact it was a Leyland design team (based at Watford) that was given the chassis design job rather than Scammell's own men, with predictably dire results. The main competitor, the Bantam, had the great advantage of having a reasonably large cab that was suitable for haulage, a feature not shared with the Atlas. Another salient point was that the Bantam had a complete chassis from front to rear, whereas the Atlas used a car-like front end complete with independent front suspension, which was then almost unknown on vehicles above 2-tons capacity.

What the Leyland design team was asked to do was to marry the Atlas front with a Scarab rear, and then make a stable 4-wheel tractor unit. The Atlas engine was canted over at an angle and bolted to the Scammell gearbox and rear axle and this combined unit located at the rear by two semi-elliptic slipper mounted leaf springs. At the front of the engine a large rubber bush had acted as the attachment point on the Scarab chassis and this same mounting was incorporated in the new vehicle. The unsprung weight of this combined unit acted rather like a huge trailing arm, and when combined with the independent front suspension it gave a bouncy ride at the higher speeds that the Atlas was able to attain. The rear of the chassis was based on the Scarab, but was all-welded with the coupling ramps integral with the chassis.

To be fair it must be pointed out that the engineers did a reasonable design job given the complete basic incompatibility of the two major components (Standard/Scammell). Added to this incompatibility was the fact that there was little money in the Experimental Department's kitty to spend a lot of time and effort on the project.

One of the few good features of this vehicle was the correct proportioning of braking effort, so that the front brakes took more of the braking effort than the unit's rear axle brakes and therefore theoretically avoided a potential jack-knife. This gave very stable braking under maximum deceleration and showed how good the engineers could be. The front brakes were uprated from the normal Atlas brakes.

Although some of the contemporary road testers were complementary about the braking standards, the foundation brakes were prone to fade badly which did nothing for consistency in braking. Further problems came with high pedal and gear lever effort being required, leading to clutch slipping to save unnecessary leg and arm movements. Another nail in the coffin of this supposed urban mini-artic was that the cab was just too small and narrow for any driver who was not small or medium size, yet in contrast the cab doors were extremely wide and somewhat of an embarrassment in narrow streets. Had this vehicle been built in the late-1940s when any new truck would sell, rather than 1962 (when buyers had a wide choice of alternatives) it might possibly have been a success. As it happened it came out on sale at a time when the small artic tractor was going out of fashion and, being inferior in almost every aspect to the competition, the Scarab 4 failed miserably! Only a handful came to be sold in Britain, and the only major customer at the time was the South African Railway who took about 60 units. Just two major aspects of this ungainly marriage did last and they were the use of the 'canted over' Leyland engine and the welded chassis in the 3-ton Scarab's replacement called the Townsman.

The demise of the Scarab and the Karrier Bantam and indeed the other small articulated units started in the early to mid-1960s when BR set about modernising their sundries collection and delivery services to cope with a disastrous loss of traffic and non-existent profitability. Many outlying depots were closed and delivery routes lengthened, so there was much less demand for the swapping of trailers during a day's work. This is a subject that has already been covered at length in the **Nostalgia Road** book *British Railways Road Vehicles 1948-68*.

At the same time overall road speeds were increasing and the 3-wheelers were geared to run at a maximum speed of about 28 mph, which was presumed to be too slow although the Bantams were faster. A further nail in the coffin of the automatic coupling followed the general uprating of vehicle gross weights with the 1964 Construction & Use Regulations. Under these new rules there was a massive jump towards 32-tonnes articulated truck operation making use of fifth wheel couplings with tandem or tri-axle trailers and giving a payload potential of 21-22-tonnes. This compared with just 12-tonnes available on the auto units. This figure of 12-tonnes was the maximum that the regulations considered safe with the automatic coupling. Thus at a stroke many of the auto couplings' inbuilt advantages were lost despite the fact that the Scammell company could boast its range of semi trailers numbering up to 600 differing versions.

The final blow was that the new Plating & Testing Regulations appeared to threaten the very existence of 3-wheel tractor units with unbraked front wheels. So developments were carried out in Scammell's Experimental Department, with a view to the possibility of building a 3-wheeler with front brakes. Various trials were carried out using brake equipment from Rootes Group cars, but it was decided not to go ahead with the plan to either build new 3-wheelers with front brakes or even to retrofit any existing vehicles. The logic behind the decision was almost certainly due to the fact that both Scammell and BR realised that the heyday of the 3-wheeler was almost over.

Above: *Looking uncannily like the real thing, this is in fact a wooden mock up of the new Scammell three wheel tractor unit that was to become the Townsman. In the days before computers and Computer Aided Design (CAD) the designers would build firstly clay and then wooden mock-ups of proposed new models. The fact that the new cab would be built in fibreglass (or glass fibre?) meant that the designers could use body panel shapes that would not be possible in metal. But would this be the vehicle to meet the needs of the 'Swinging Sixties'?* Mechanical Horse Club.

Below: *The Karrier Walk-thru was a popular choice for delivery vans within BR's Rail Express operation. In the early-1960s one chassis was fitted with an automatic coupling for use in trials as a possible Scarab replacement. The vehicle was really too big for the intended job and no more was heard of this idea.*

CHAPTER 11. THE FINAL FLING

Above: *The TW9, the last stage in the Mechanical Horse story.*

Despite the introduction of the new Construction & Use regulations that were to change the face of road transport in Great Britain, the Scammell management were asked by British Railways to produce an up-dated 3-wheel tractor unit that would operate into the 1970s on specific railway 'smalls' delivery services. The outcome was the Townsman (a 5-ton capacity 3-wheeler based on the Scarab 3-tonner) which featured a new diesel engine, better rear brakes and improved driver comfort.

The first Townsman appeared in 1964 and was fitted with a stylish new glass reinforced plastic cab, which was initially built by Reliant in Tamworth and later at the Thornycroft works in Basingstoke. This vehicle also made use of the all-welded chassis first seen in the Scarab 4, rather than the bolted chassis used successfully by Scammells in the past. This new fangled idea proved at the time to be the Achilles Heel of both the Scarab 4 and the Townsman, as it was found that the nearside chassis members were cracking with monotonous regularity. A larger engine based on the Standard/Leyland OE160 62bhp diesel was the only option and vacuum brakes over hydraulic brakes were specified to give a higher standard of braking. Despite the provision of a fixed driver's seat, different size drivers could be accommodated by the simple expedient of moving the pedal cluster backwards and forwards.

In 1964 the Townsman replaced the 3-ton Scarab although production of the 6-ton Scarab continued until 1967. The new Townsman attracted an order for 50 from British Railways in 1964, and a further 1,290 in 1965. They were also bought by the GPO and a number of orders from smaller users. An improvement over the earlier 3-wheeler was the Townsman's steering wheel, which was not quite as vertically mounted as that on the Scarab since universal joints were incorporated into the steering column. The air intake for the radiator was positioned on top of the cab roof under the registration plate and air was carried by trunking down the cab rear panel into the radiator. But sadly the day of the 3-wheel tractor unit was passing. There was nothing wrong with the basic concept it was just that times had changed.

Modern, mass produced trucks in the 4- to 10-ton range could match many of the better points of the 3-wheel tractor units, they were cheaper to buy and economics made the provision of specialised, under utilised trailers a difficult purchase to justify. Despite the changes in the ground rules one other manufacturer did enter the 3-wheel market about 1965 and that was the Reliant Company. They had commissioned Ogle Design of Letchworth to design a vehicle (the TW9 seen above) that could move part-completed car chassis from one part of the factory to another.

Some articulated versions of this 3-wheeler came to be seen in use with a number of municipal operators, as a tractor coupled to a semi low load trailer capable of carrying parks department equipment. Production later passed to BTB in Oswaldtwistle near Accrington (Lancashire) and was named the Ant, while a large number were exported and others were built abroad under licence. A small batch came to be bought by the Isle of Man Steam Packet Company as replacements for time expired Scarabs and Townsmen that had been bought new or second-hand.

In order to face up to the new Plating & Testing Regulations, Scammell introduced a conversion kit to enable fifth wheel trailers to couple easily to their Auto coupling tractors. The kit consisted of a fifth wheel attached to a cross-member, which could either remain on the tractor unit or on the trailer or be transferred between other tractors and trailers. All of the conversions involved single axle trailers, and both National Carriers and BRS Parcels made use of this equipment.

While this was a short term measure many users of auto couplings changed completely to fifth wheel couplings, often converting existing trailers as the tractor units were renewed. Eventually the conversions were phased out as the rapid move to tandem and tri-axle trailers took place and the last two major users of auto-couplings, National Carriers and Roadline merged and reappeared as Lynx Express. Many of their 28ft long auto-coupling vans were rebuilt into tandem axle, single tyred box vans fitted with fifth wheel couplings. It appeared that by the 1990s the auto coupling had breathed its last; yet in 1999 the British Army still used Bedford TL tractor units fitted with Tasker style couplings.

Back in the 1930s the French firm of Chernard et Walcker were building Scammell Mechanical Horses and automatic couplings under licence. Eventually the FAR Company took up production of the 3-wheelers and later built a 4-wheel version, which could properly be described as an urban artic. These later models used a Saviem cab, which improved the drivers' comfort. The French Company really took the urban artic concept further than the Leyland group ever did, and their 1950s and 1960s models featured 3-wheel braking, initially hydraulic and later air actuated. Two-speed rear axles were the norm and there was automatic coupling of the air brakes. Even the cabs would tilt to allow repairs and servicing! In the mid-1990s some of the four wheelers were still working in Paris as urban delivery vehicles for Marks & Spencer. Perhaps there is a moral here? At the start of the 21st century no 3-wheelers are known to be in regular commercial use, although a Sussex firm is still using auto-coupling trailers for the internal movement of part-completed furniture between its works. In this instance the trailers are hauled by Ford 'D' series tractors.

As stated at the outset, this story had a beginning, middle and an end, but the end forms quite another story, and will be the subject of a future book. The early years saw the introduction of a very successful replacement for the horse on delivery work. The concept of automatic coupling spread to the hard pressed road hauliers who took up the concept with a great deal of enthusiasm by allowing them to handle loads more efficiently. The Mechanical Horse and its close relatives must surely rank amongst the greatest as examples of vehicles built for a specific task and able to perform it in a most exemplary manner!

Above: *There is much more to say about the latter years of the Mechanical Horse concept, and we promise to return to the subject in a future volume. Despite all the problems associated with plating and testing for the 3-wheelers they continued to operate in many areas for a further 20 years. Several found employment as works hacks, others continued in their original role of short distance shunting of trailers.*

Below: *On the Isle of Man, the Steam Packet Company put them to good use for many years and they purchased the TW 9 load carrier which was employed on a variety of duties between the company's ferry terminal in Douglas Harbour, and other points on the island. They also purchased both new and second hand Scammell Townsman as seen here with MN3449.*

The final British Railway operation of the Scammells and indeed the Karrier Bantams and Ford's baby artics finished with the closing of the Rail Express operation in the early-1980s.

IN CONCLUSION

Despite its demise, the mechanical horse has not completely disappeared for a wide variety of models have been preserved. The National Railway Museum in York has a very early LMS Karrier Cob in its original form, along with an early 3-ton LNER tractor, a later GWR 6-ton Mechanical Horse and a BR Morrison electric 'horse. Meanwhile a large number of privately-owned 'horses (of all varieties) can be seen during the summer season attending the rallies and shows across the country.

There is a club catering for enthusiasts of this unique concept, which was formed in 1983 and brought together a number of like-minded enthusiasts who had been exchanging notes for some time. A bi-monthly news sheet is issued, and this covers the latest information on vehicle movements, discovery of hitherto unknown 'horses in scrapyards, vehicles, trailers and spares for sale and wanted, as well as special features, rally reports, articles and photographs. This is the Mechanical Horse Club.

The club can be contacted via the membership secretary, Brian Madeley, whose address appears at the front of this book: If any reader is aware of any auto-coupling tractors or trailer units still in use could they please contact the Mechanical Horse Club.

A lot of help in getting this book off the ground was given freely by members of the Mechanical Horse Club, including: Paul Bourne, John Downes, Brian Madeley, Sean Madeley, Peter Newman, David Smith and David Wood amongst many others. Most of the information on the introduction of the Karrier models came from Ken Millet and I am very grateful for his help on this particular matter.

In many ways though the most important contributor has been the founder of the Mechanical Horse Club, Geoff Arnold. His ability in forming the Club resulted in more people being made aware of these vehicles, which in turn led to the rescue and preservation of many 3-wheelers that would otherwise have been lost. Without his help this book (and indeed the vehicle preservation scene) would have been much poorer.